Interior Colour Palettes

PAGE ONE

目录 CONTENTS

163 **Chapter Three: Interior Colour Scheme**

PREFACE

The World Outside

Nobody knows if there are distinct colours in this world. The world is perceived differently by the various life forms. We recognise the beauty in colours and the kaleidoscope of them that surrounds us—a juxtaposition of colours created by objects, light and our eyes.

The World Inside

People build homes and often, they attempt to bring the splendours of the outdoor to the indoor. Many today can enjoy the beauty of colours in the comfort of their homes, unlike those in the past. A century ago, colour televisions, colour-printed books and magazines, and coloured fabrics were unheard of. Colours were flavours of the rich and they symbolised wealth.

The People Inside

To most in the room, the culture behind the Roman poles and the beauty implied in winding spaces do not hold much significance. However, colours do. The resplendent gleam of gold, the serenity of blue, the passion of red and the vitality of green—they all add life to the monotonous and stir our emotions.

The Designers

Designers are professionals in the use of colours. Using colours, they change the shape and size of spaces; cover 'faults'; harmonise objects; and create ambiences.

The Interior Colour Design

Chapter One:
The General Rules of Colours in Interior Design

Colours have a greater impact on the human vision than the variation of shapes. This is particularly so for those without professional knowledge of colour use. The use of colours directly affects the overall impression of a space communicated by the interior design.

Classification of Interior Colours

The various colours in a space come together to put up some kind of a soap opera: walls play lead roles, furniture take centre stage, lights usher latecomers, and plants become props. In a line, different colours tell different stories. Put in good order by the hands of designers, colours harmonise to define spaces.

According to their purpose and extent, colours are categorised into three groups: Main Colours, Accent (Key) Colours, and Colours for Touch.

Main Colours

←

The main colour refers to the colour which takes up a larger space in a room. They include the floor, walls, ceiling and large partition walls.

The main colour is considered the main tone of a room's colour scheme. In most cases, the main colours comprise those in the grey series which promote a harmonious setting. Vibrant main colours create deeper first impressions.

←

Red, the main colour, defines the cream-coloured sofa.

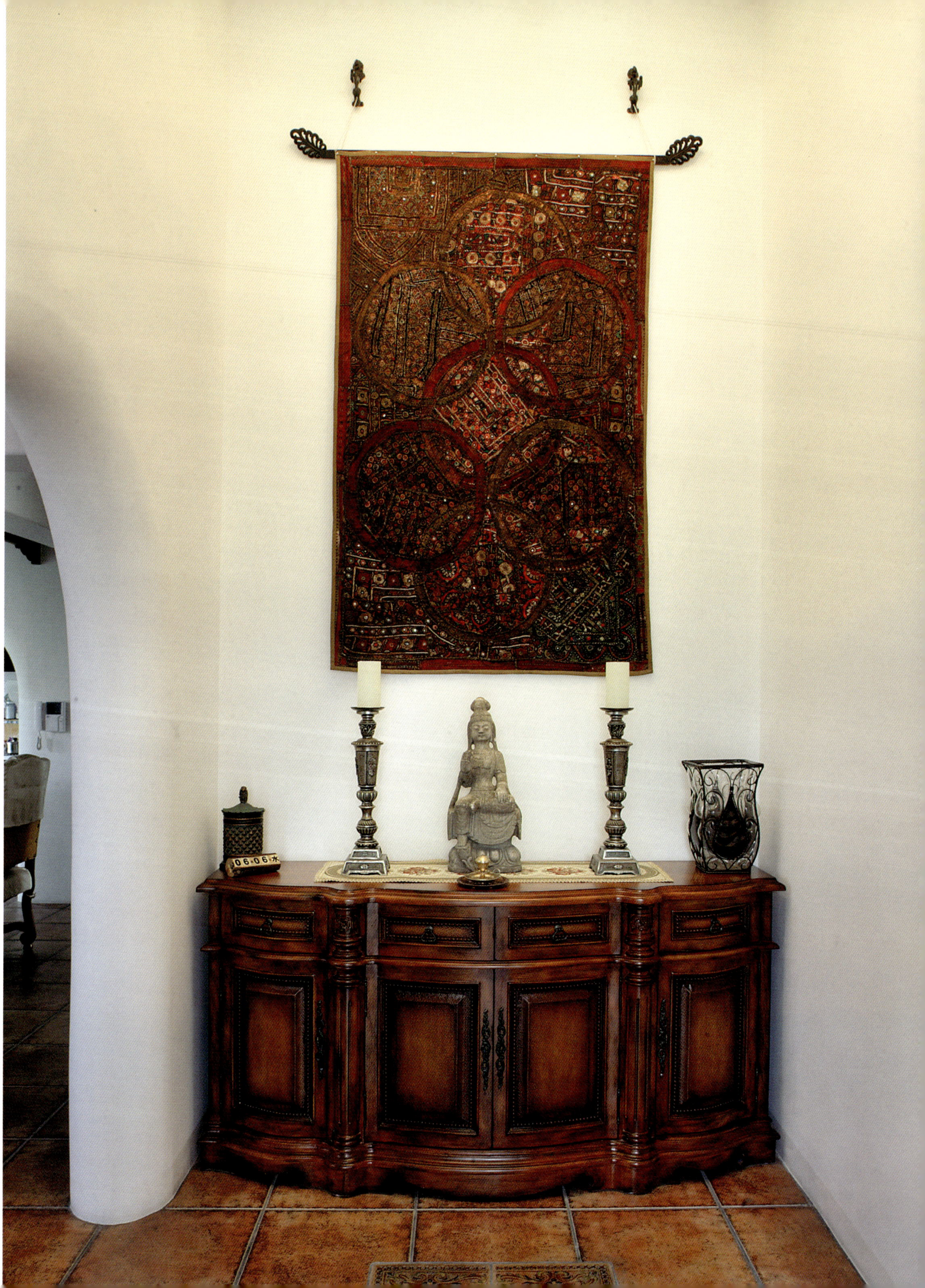
06·06

←
The accent color gives a deep impression.

Accent Colours

←

The accent colours, the main focus of a room, come from larger pieces of furniture or indoor furnishings such as the sofa, wardrobe, table and big statues or ornaments.

There are two ways of matching main colours with accent colours. To achieve contrast, colours contrasting with or complementing main colours are chosen as the accent colours. On the other hand, to achieve harmony, colours close to the main colours such as monochromatic or analogous colours are chosen as the accent colours.

↗

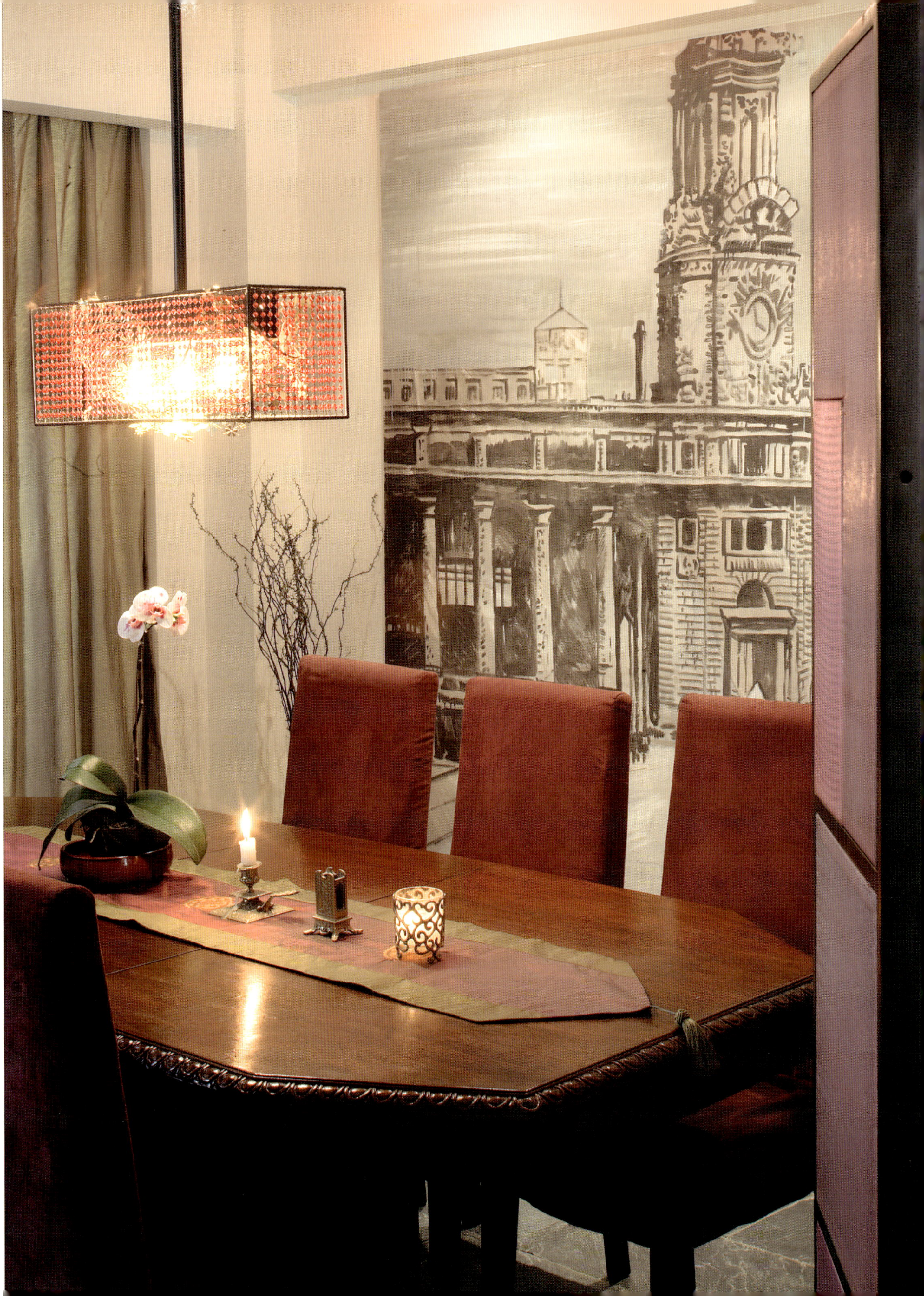

Colors for Touch

Colours for touch refer to the colours of small objects in a room. They include lights, artifacts and other soft furnishings.

Colours for touch are needed to break the monotony in the room. Thus, colours contrasting with the main colours are often chosen. If applied correctly, these colours play important roles in giving the overall design a dramatic touch. However, they are often considered insignificant and thus, are neglected.

←
Red and purple are used as the colours for touch, and put together with green for contrast.

The main colour, the primary colour used in the room, provides a platform for the other colours. Generally, it should suit the functionality of the room although sometimes, the walls and ceiling are in accent colours. Colours of low chroma and high grey are chosen to add stability to the space.

The accent colour—the melody of the room—reflects the characteristics, sets the atmosphere and creates the mood. It is defined by the main colour and together, define the colours for touch. In smaller rooms, the accent colour is close to and blends with the main colour to make the rooms appear more spacious. In larger rooms, the accent colour and the colours for touch enhance the main colour, making the rooms appear more spacious.

The role of the colours for touch is to communicate the relationships of the various colours used. The clever choice of colours for touch gives graduation and contrast, and it is the key to an outstanding design.

← The miracle of colours for touch — contrasting colours become analogous once the orange cushion is replaced by a green one.

←

The light colour of the parterre blends in with the uniform main colour while the deep colour of the handrails contrasts with the main colour.

→

In most cases, the colours for touch contrast with the accent colours.

Generally, the focus of interior design is the accent colour. A clever match of the main and accent colour—with harmony and contrast—will make the accent colour the centre of attention.

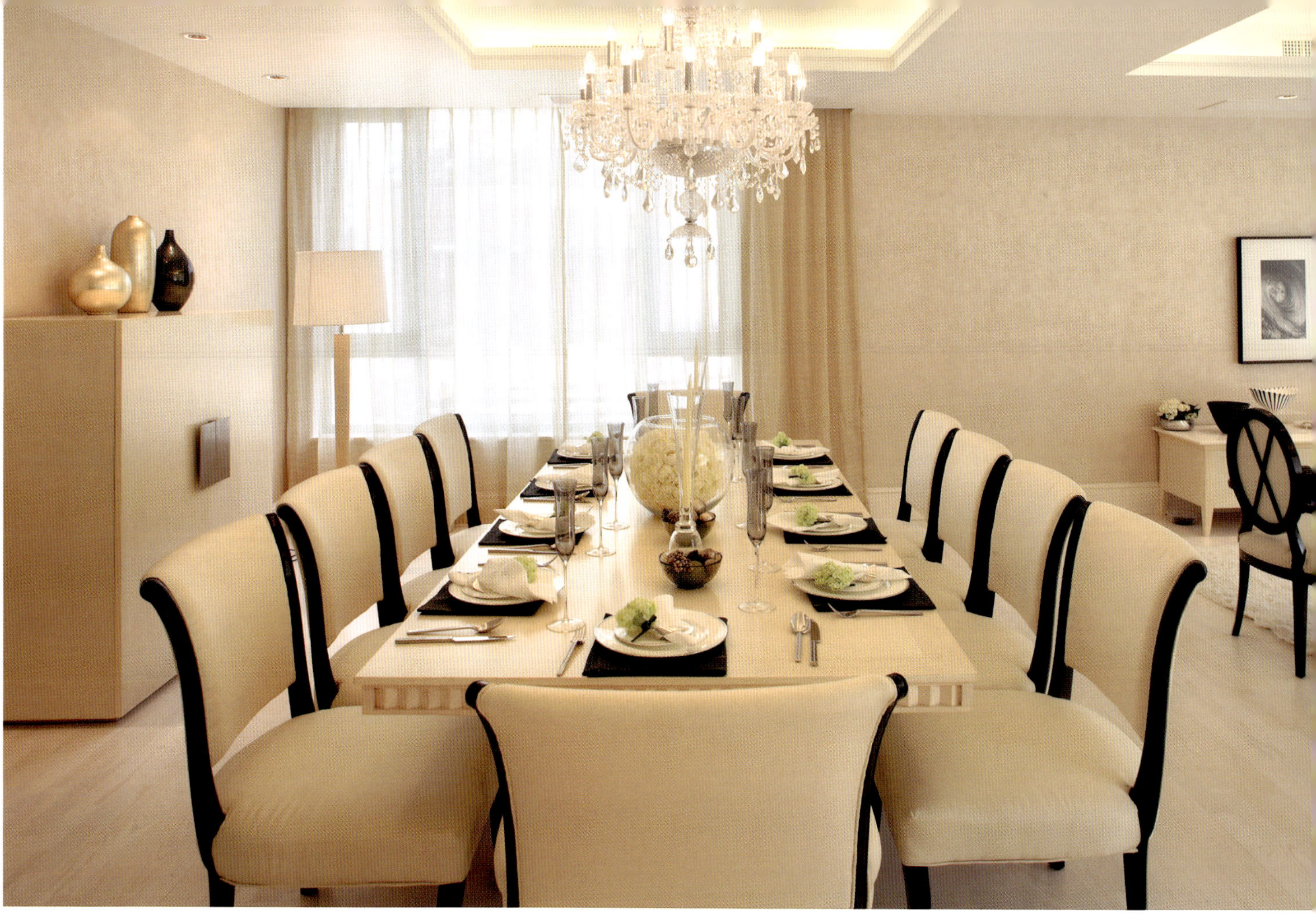

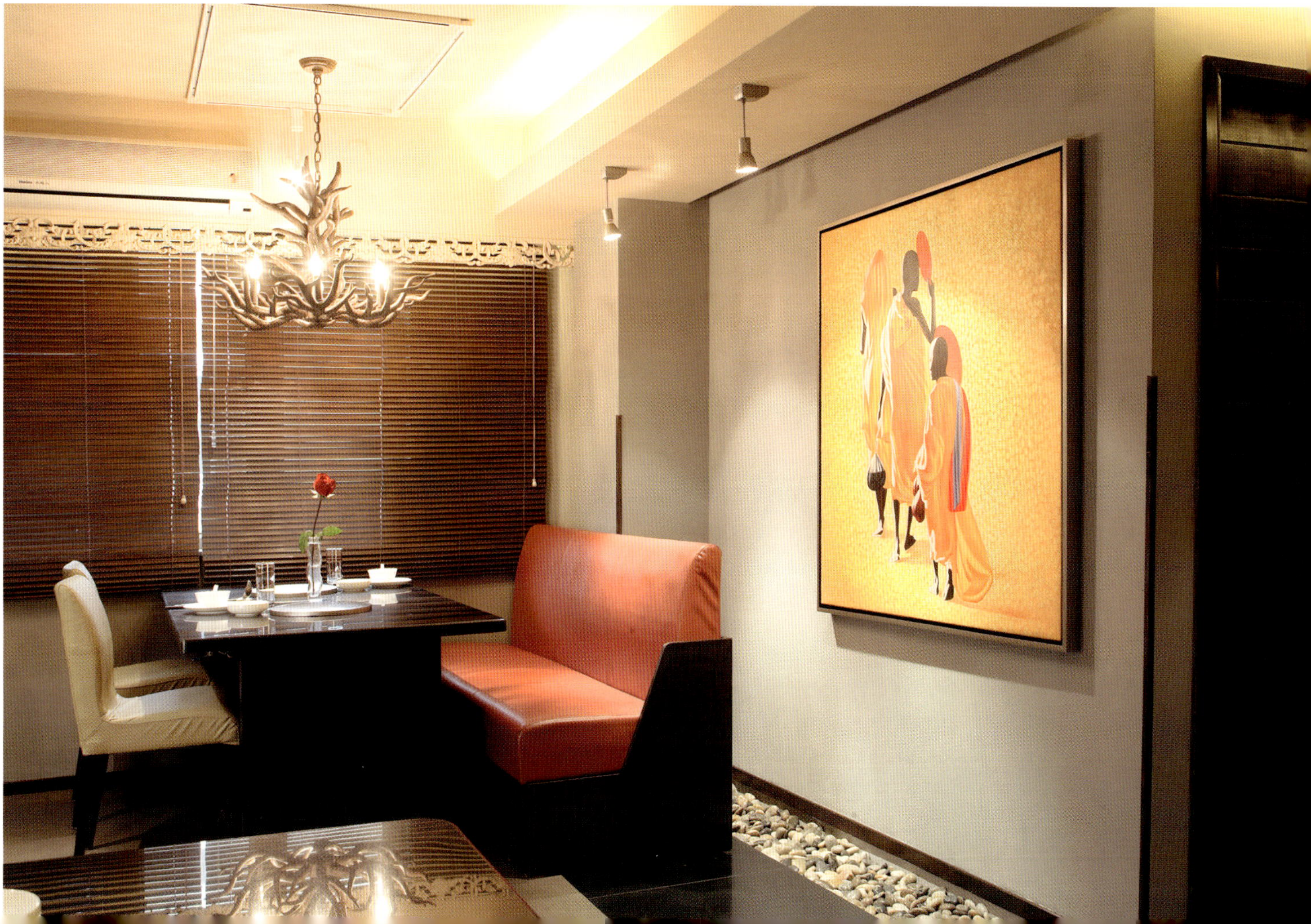

Colours and the Interior Space

In interior design, colours can change the size of a space. They do not physically alter the space, but visually modify it instead. Do not underestimate this ability as it can virtually add or reduce space in a room. This ability works on the human psychological make up, affecting perception.

The property of colours

Colours of high saturation and low brightness create a sense of forwardness and are called advancing colours. In contrast, colours of low saturation and high brightness are called receding colours.

The weight of colours

Deep colours create a sense of depression while light colours create a sense of bulge.

The expansion and reduction effects of colours

Warm colours excite the retina and the objects in view appear larger than reality. On the contrary, cool colours make the objects appear smaller. In the same grey setting, white gives a sense of expansion while black gives sense of reduction.

The following are some techniques on how to use colours to change the visual sense of space in a room.

- Cool and light colours expand the sense of space; reducing the contrast of colours also has the same effect.
- Contrasting strong, warm, deep and bright colours with other colours can reduce the sense of space. The same goes for increasing contrast betweens the colours.
- A narrow corridor will appear shorter and wider with warm or deep colours used on the walls at its furthest end.
- A small room will appear longer if the wall on the furthest end is in cool, light or grey colours. A reduction in the contrast of colours also has the same effect.
- Saturated warm colours such as creamy yellow, apricot, or light blue are chosen for dark rooms.
- Dark colours absorb light, and a touch of green or deep red will create an intimate space with character.
- The room will appear more spacious if all the surfaces — the ceiling, floor and walls — are in the same colour. Reduce the chromatism of the colours if the same colour cannot be applied.

↑

The corridor appears more spacious in light colours; the golden yellow expands the space of it.

← ←

The room appears more spacious
if all the surfaces are of the same
colour.

- If there are obtrusive features in a room, the colours of the room will camouflage them.
- For a larger space with several rooms, having each in a different colour will reduce the spaciousness. Attention should be paid to the points where the colours meet. Ensure that the various colours, textures and patterns work well together.
- For small rooms, choose a palette of colours of various intensities and vitiate them with different textures and patterns.
- Too many pieces of large furniture will make a room appear crowded and disorganised. The contrary happens when the furniture are the same colour as the main colour.
- For a room with little furnishings, dark and warm colours will make the room appear more furnished that it actually is.

↘

← Deep-coloured ceilings give a sense of depression and strengthen the relationship they have with the floor.

Measures can be taken to lower the ceiling. They include using warm or deep colours, using colours deeper than the wall colours, adding a cornice in deeper colour than the wall colours, and painting dados in colours deeper the wall colours.

The ceiling will appear higher in cool or light colours, or with a deep top stitch.

→

→ Ceiling lights increase the distance between the ceiling and the floor, making the room appear more spacious.

■ Colours lighter than the wall colours for ceilings make the white cornice stand out.

■ For a room with walls and ceiling in light colours, contrasting colour paints for the moulding makes it all better.

■ For spacious monotonous spaces, put furniture of dark brown, some large plants, big flower baskets or pottery to add a touch of individualism.

■ Want the room to have a radiant glow? Paint it in colours! On the contrary, a dark flooring will make the room appear smaller and serious.

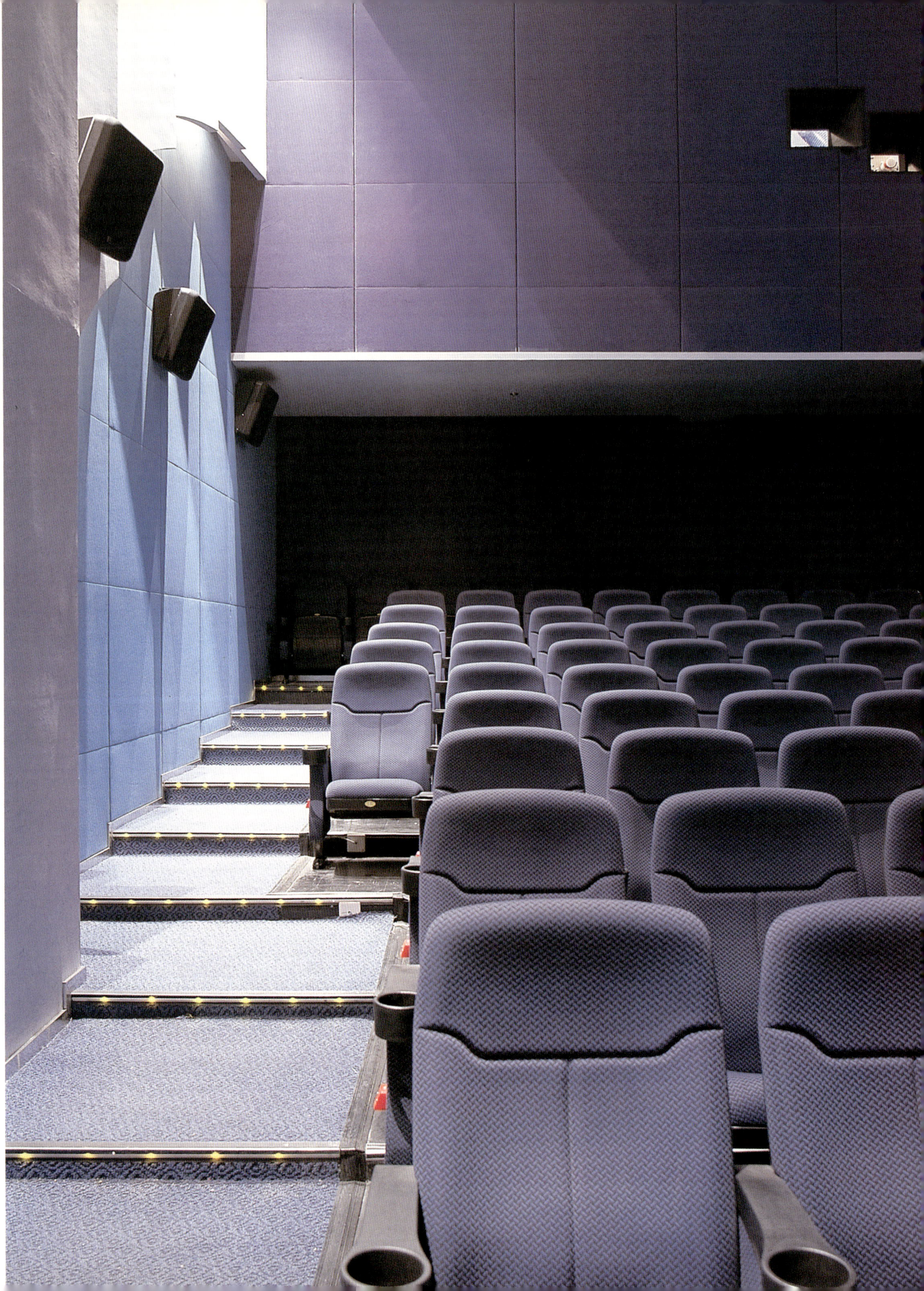

Colours and the Interior Lighting

Natural Light

Sunlight is full spectrum and has been used in artistic environments for correct colour perception. This kind of light not only allows the human eye to see colours better but also details more clearly in a natural way. The human eye can see colours of visible spectrum of 400nm to 700nm, including red, orange, yellow, greens, blue, indigo, violet and their subtle variations.

Natural light is best for viewing nature. The colours of nature are very rich and only natural light can fully display their variations-even the best printer in the world cannot replicate their subtle variations such as the coloured veins of a fallen leaf.Nature's good craftsmanship is what distinguishes natural from artificial light.

Natural light is imperative in residential homes, educational institutions, hospitals, factories, etc.

←
The magic of coloured lights in a theatre.

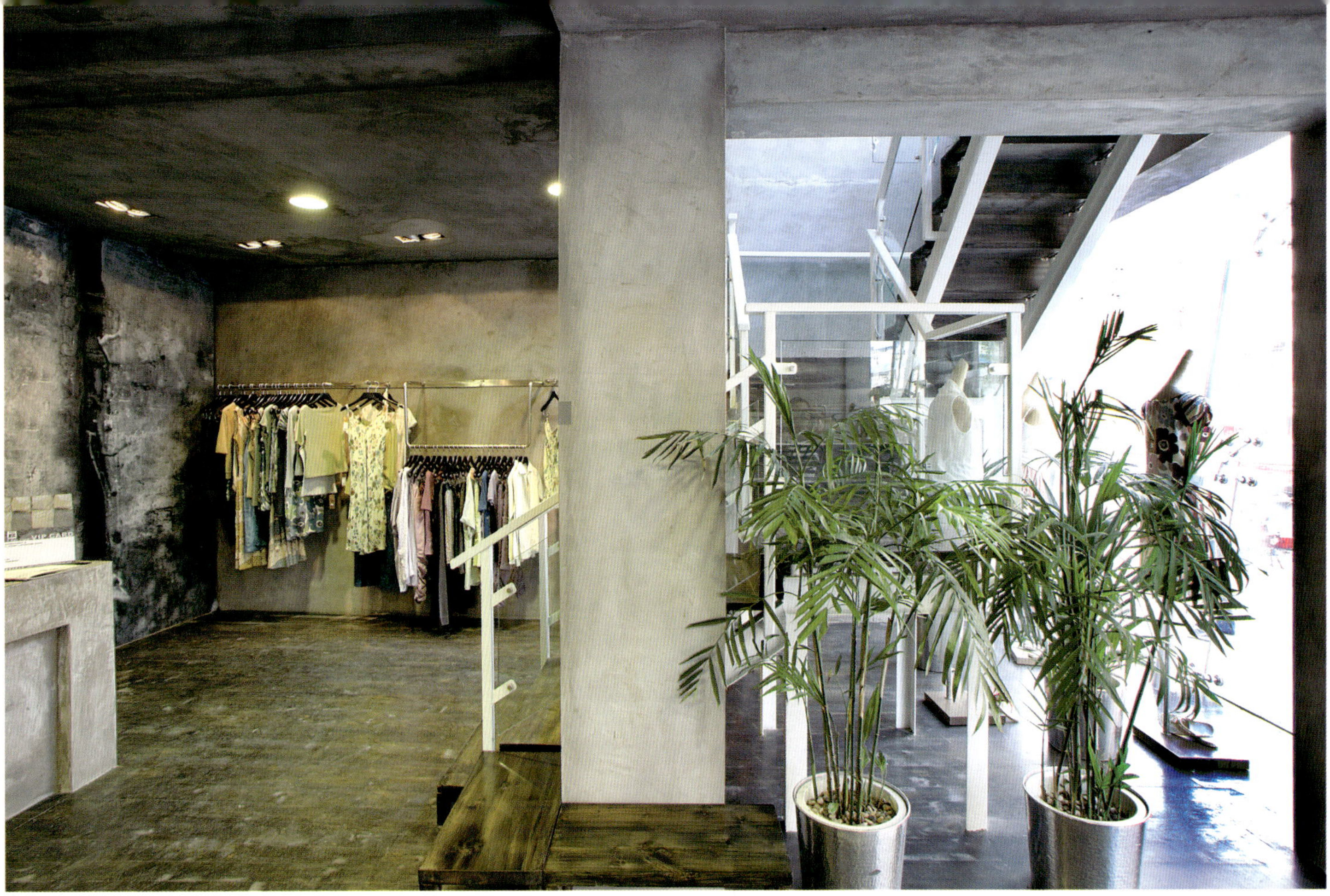

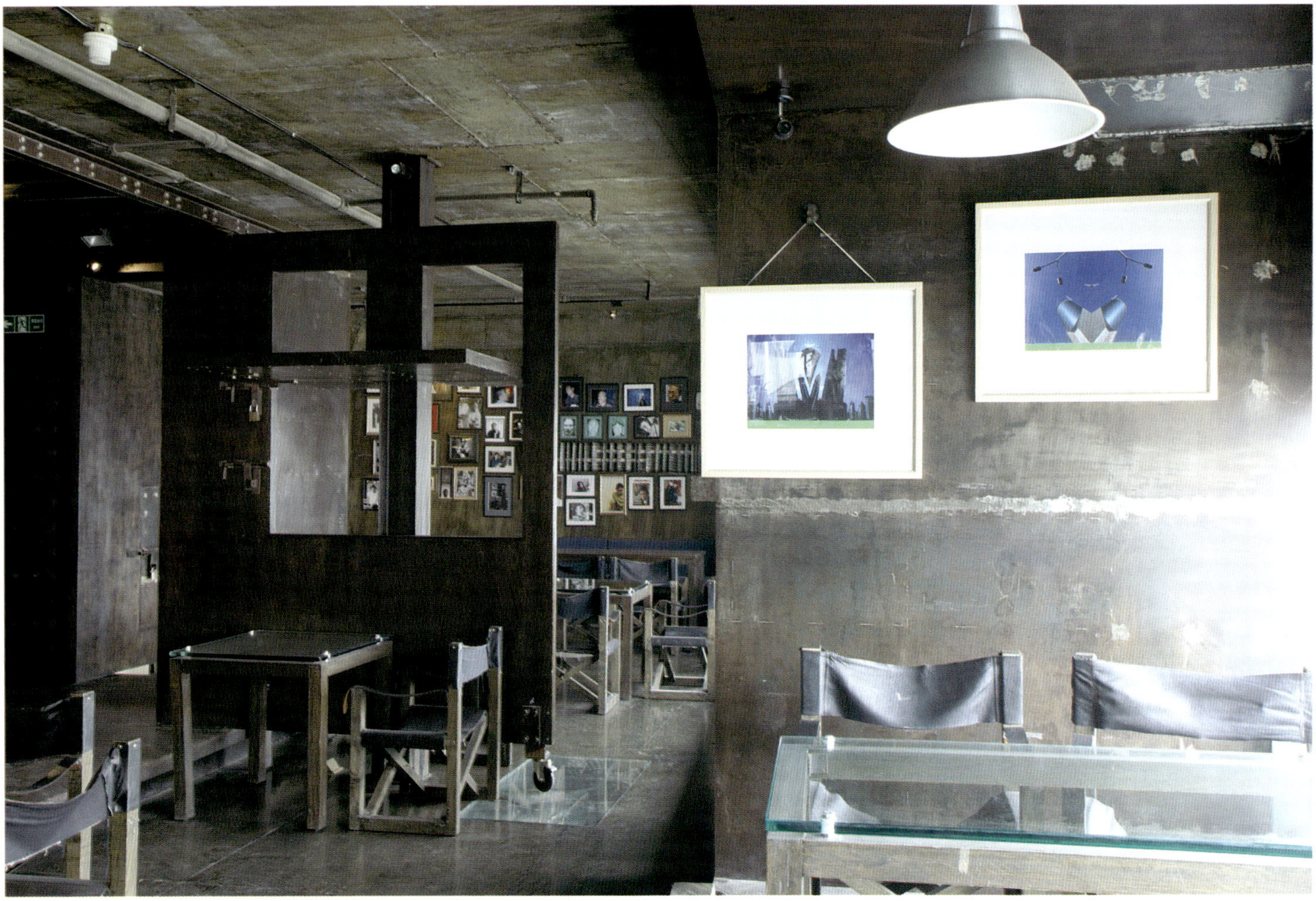

The same colour and texture of a space appear different in natural and artificial light.

Natural light can enhance different interior styles. It is very easy for designers to match colours in natural light as the latter illuminates objects exactly. Natural light is particularly indispensable to rooms with many live plants.

Natural colours are exceptional. They change with the seasons: strong and hot in summer; cool and weak in winter; clear and bright in spring; and weak and cool in autumn. The weather also affects natural light-bluish on clear days, yellowish in the sunshine, and reddish at dawn. Moonlight has a poor colouration. It is difficult to distinguish warm colours like red or orange and thus, blue-violet is often used to show night scenes. Also, the chroma and lighting angles of natural light vary with time.

The lighting here is uniquh — che coloured cups complement the effect of silhouettes cast.

Artificial light

Humans differ from animals in that we enjoy life both in the day and night. However, our biological make up promotes greater activity in the day and this explains why our eyes cannot see as well at night. Thus, it is necessary to create a visible world at night with artificial lighting.

Artificial lights imitate sunlight. Although there is a wide range of artificial lighting, none can compare to natural light due to the lighting principles it works on. And this is why artificial lights have their limitations: the incandescent lamp is yellow, the fluorescent lamp is slightly blue, high or low halogen lights are yellow, the mercury lamp appears blue when cold, and the multi-steam lamp is green when cold. These lights not only vary in colour, but also in their reducing power; the incandescent lamp, unlike the fluorescent lamp, shows warm colours well and deviates when lighting cool colours.

The restoring power of colours is generally referred to as Ra (Colour Rendering Index). Lights between Ra 89 to 100 can reflect the true colours of objects while those below Ra 50 will produce colour cast or cause visual damage. Another index to show the rendering property of colour is colour temperature. Ordinary incandescent lamps have a lower temperature than natural light and thus, may warm lit objects while mercury lights have a higher temperature and thus, make objects appear cold.

← ←
Coloured lights greatly change the original characteristics of colours.

Although the colours deviate and are not as strong as in the day, they are adequate for dark rooms and underground places. For some places such as art galleries, museums and exhibitions, which emphasise lighting, special colours with high-colour rendering properties should be chosen. For educational and commercial spaces such as classrooms, lecture theatres, libraries and offices, energy-saving lights with high temperatures should be used. Lastly, for places which do not need to show the original colours of the objects in them but dramatic touches to create certain ambience, colours of extreme temperatures should be chosen. Places of such include coffee bars, dance halls and discotheques.

Henhale's table of mixed colours

Light colours	Red	Orange	Yellow	Yellow-green	Green	Dark green	Black
Violet	Purplish red	Dark red	Pale red	White	Ondink	Reddish black	Blue
Blue	Dark Red	Pale red	White	Ondink	Reddish black	Reddish black	
Black	Pale red	White	Ondink	Ondink	Dark green		
Dark green	White	Pale yellow	Ondink	Green			
Green	Pale yellow	Yellow	Yellow-green				
Yellow-green	Golen yellow	Yellow					
Yellow	Orange						

Colours of Lights

The reflection of light on a large space of a single colour affects the surrounding objects.

Just as artificial lights can be of single colours, natural full spectrum light too can be changed into coloured lights with the use of coloured glass. Many unique designs with rose windows or tempered glass make use of this technique. The folding of light colours and the colours of objects follows the subtractive colour mix principle. This is the same as mixing the colour of lights with the colour of objects. For example, when red light falls on white objects, the objects will appear red, and when red light falls on green objects, the objects will appear black. The folding of the colours of lights follows the additive colour mixture principle: red and green lights give yellow light, and red and blue lights give violet light. The brightness of the resultant light is the total brightness of all the lights.

Many easily apply the subtractive colour mixture principle based on their own experiences. However, when dealing with a mixture of chromatic lights, it is advisable to seek professional lighting designers. The mixture of light and colours is of special importance to the design of stages, dance halls and discotheques. As lights and colours are more and more widely used in modern designs, the explorations in this field gain greater recognition.

The same set of setting appears cold with cold lights.

Colours and Textures

In the real world, colours will neither appear abstract nor absolute. They have apparent textures to the eye. The difference in textures lies in their patterns and surfaces.

The smallest difference can produce an extraordinary result. Someone, in an experiment, showed a group of women a piece of stained silk and a piece of spun silk. Although the two pieces of silk are of the same colour, most of the women thought otherwise. This difference stems from the tactile appearance of the two materials: stain silk, smooth in outlook, is associated with cold metals or mirrors and its colour thus appears cool while spun silk, coarser in outlook, is associated with wooden materials or furs and its colour thus appears warm. The rough or smooth surface of materials apparently affects a person's perception of colours. This behaviour is called 'The Visual-Tactile-Sense'. The principles of Visual-Tactile-Sense are presented in the following sections.

Cool and Warm

Metals, glass, stones, mirrors and water are good conductors of heat and thus, give a sense of coolness. Weaves and furs, on the other hand, are considered warm materials while wood is considered warmer than metals and glass but colder than weaves and furs. In light of these, people are inclined to associate tactile senses with colours of materials. However, when red appears on an iron board or orange appears on stones, these colours predominate. The contrast, established by the warm colours against the coolness of the materials, reduces the warm effect of the colours. Similarly, the cool effect of the materials weakens against the warm colours.

Roughness and Smoothness

The surface of materials vary from one to another, even materials of the same kind. An example is the granite. A polished granite has a smooth surface with clear veins and colour while a frosted granite has an uneven surface with low-value chroma.

The more uneven the surface of a material, the more different its colour appears. Many Modernist designers today limit the number of colour schemes to show space and white is the predominant colour used. However, they emphasise greatly on the use of different textures. With the application of different textures and processing techniques, the same colour will show rich yet subtle variations. For pure white, the coarser the surface, the lower the value. On the contrary, the smoother the surface, the more reflective the colour. This relationship determines the variations of value and saturation of colours.

Generally, the random scattering of light on rough surfaces reduces the saturation of a colour. However, it is different for value. In most cases, when made rough, a light-coloured smooth surface will appear darker, and a dark-coloured smooth surface will appear lighter.

←

← The same colour appears different on stones, wallpapers and dopes.

↘ Wood grains, bamboo weaves and furs agree on both colour and texture.

→

Veins

Veins refer to the patterns, colours and tactile senses. Nature has a vast store of veins, but they are usually difficult to replicate. The spectacular effects of these veins bring about visual pleasure. The tactile senses of the veins do not translate to people's perception of them. The veins offer people visual imagination. For example, when composite flooring of the same smoothness and colour are used with Manchurian ash or oak, the rich curves of the Manchurian ash and straight veins of the oak will affect the colours.

The fine and delicate veins of the Manchurian ash will brighten and strengthen the colours.In contrast, the rustic and loose veins of the oak will darken the colours. Different treatment of the veins of the Manchurian ash and oak will affect the expression of colours. As with similar polished crafts in wood furnishings, the veins appear brighter and clearer in bright paints than flat varnishes.

↓

The linen screen is set against the wall and serves as a setting for the red satin.

The lights highlight the texture of the rough plain wall.

The plain cement walls and ceiling
exacerbates the rustic feel of the
space.

←
Large furnishings can be the accent colours which are the primary focus.

Colours and Furnishings

Interior furnishings refer to objects such as fabrics, statues and ornaments used to enhance the decoration of a space.

Large Furnishings

Large furnishings are the focus of a room in terms of spacialty and impression. They represent the accent colours of the room and play a vital role in the colour scheme. In view of such a function, large furnishings are positioned in key areas of the room: in front of the main wall, in the centre of the room, and in the core of activities. They are sometimes used to convert a space and are placed at the entrance of a lift or corridor. Large furnishings also enhance the thematic and sensual significance of a space. They should be in harmony with the surroundings, yet stand out as the key focus.

There are two types of colour scheme for large furnishings:

1.Harmonious scheme:For a harmonious colour scheme for large furnishings, choose colours in accordance with the main colour and give prominence by increasing contrast of value.

2.Contrasting scheme:For a contrasting scheme, choose complementary or contrasting colours to the main colours to define the cool and warm, or dark and bright.

←

The coloured furnishings create
a clean and neat environment.

Medium-sized Furnishings

Medium-sized furnishings are small and less prominent. The general rule is to harmonise them
with the style of the room and reduce contrast.

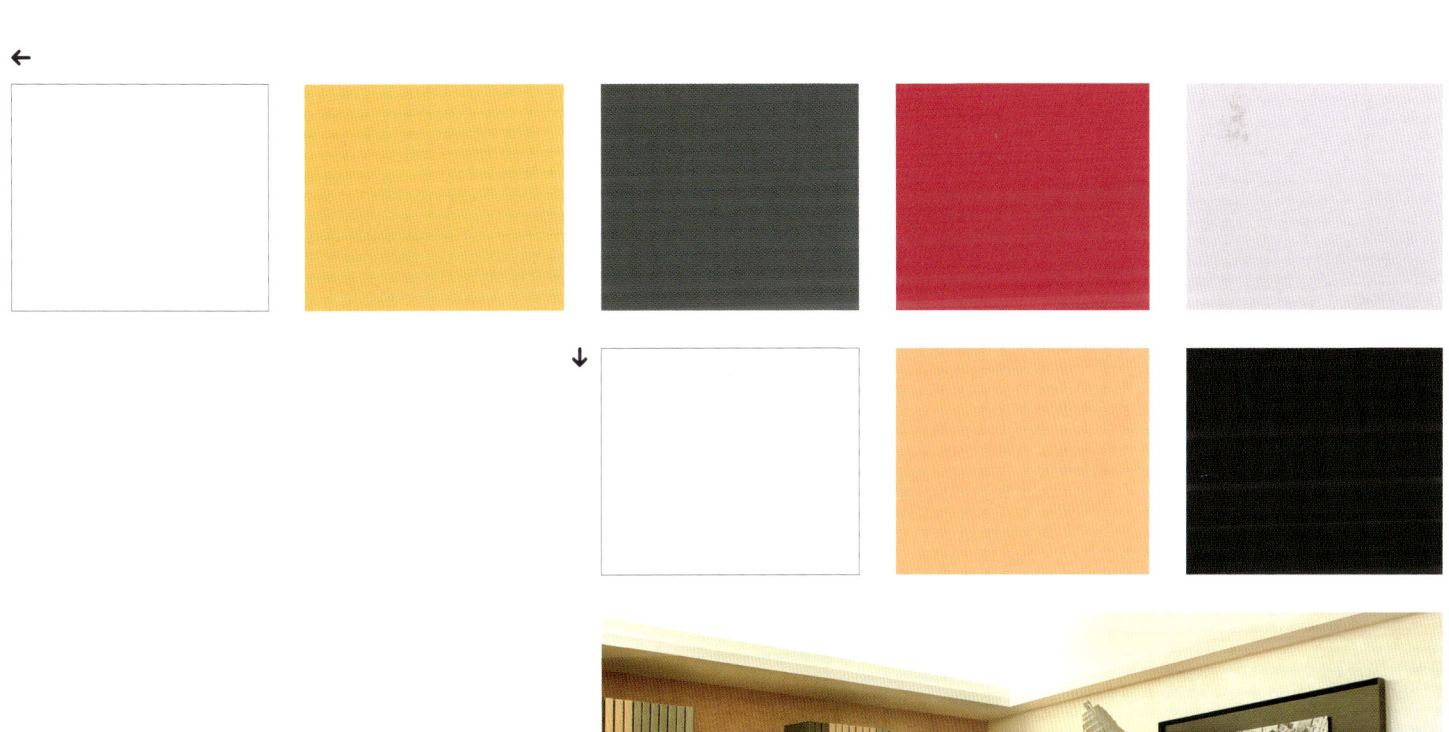

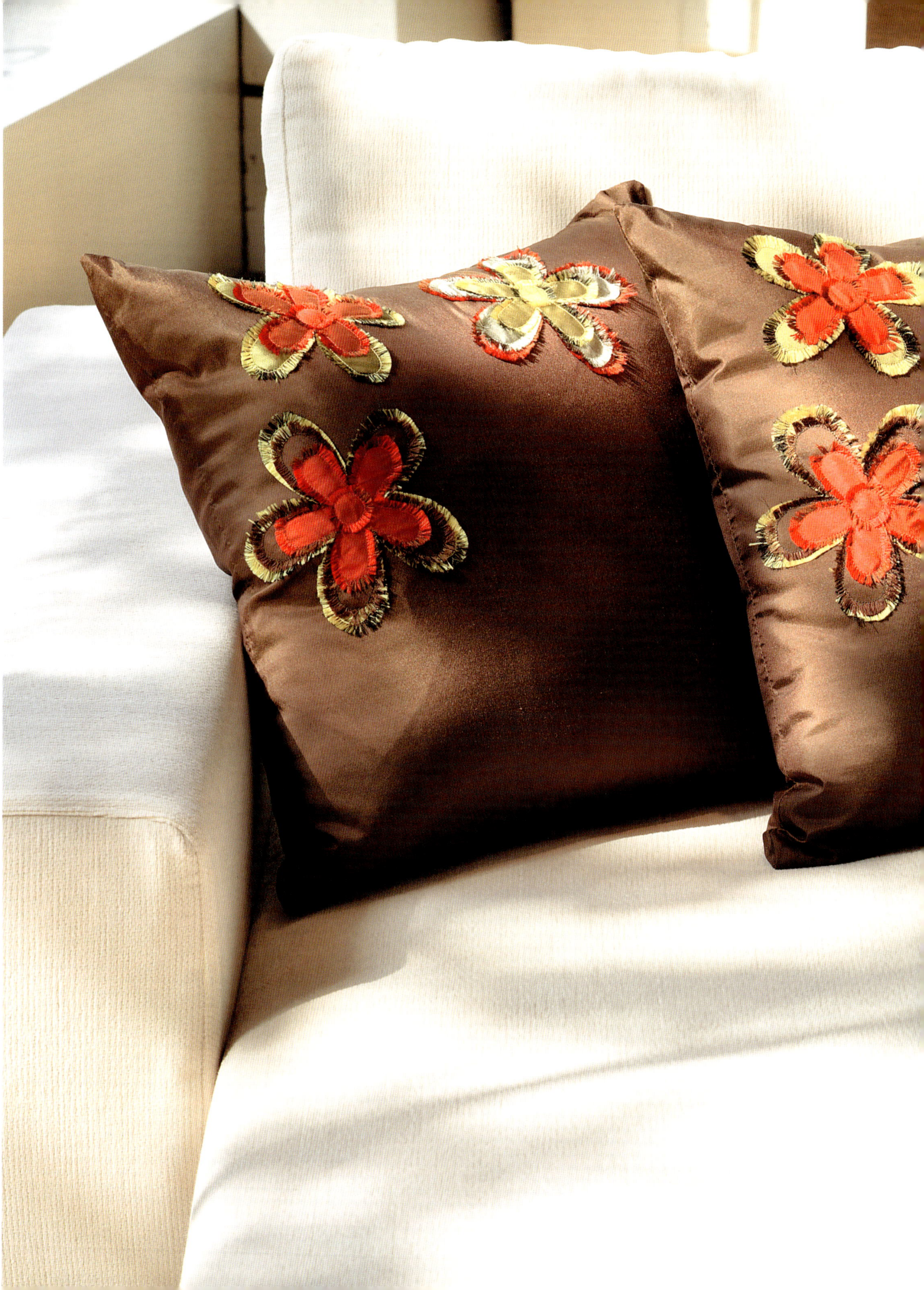

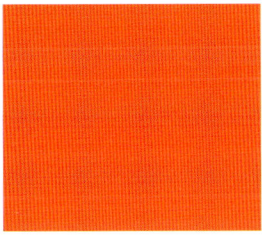

Small Furnishings

Small furnishings are the details of a room and because of their size, they will not affect the overall colour scheme. In many cases, they add life to the room when bright, complementary or contrasting colours to the main colours are used. They also enrich the effects of colour in the room. Of course, when the colours in the room are rich and contrasting, we can choose either types of colour for the small furnishings. There is trick we can adopt for such a case. For example, in a red-green scheme, choose some small red or green ornaments and place the green ones before the red setting and vice versa. This way, each colour is placed together with the opposing colour and this gives rise to graduation of red and green.

Small red flowers on the cushions brings warmth to the room.

Soft Furnishings

There are two magicians who hold the reigns of magic of colours in interior design: lights and soft furnishings. Artificial light changes the expression of colours quickly while natural light varies the colour, brightness and feel of a room with changes in days and seasons. Soft furnishings also share the same ability.

← Playing with rich colours, the green lampshades, yellow silk curtains and the purple drapes introduce change to the space to create a whole new world.

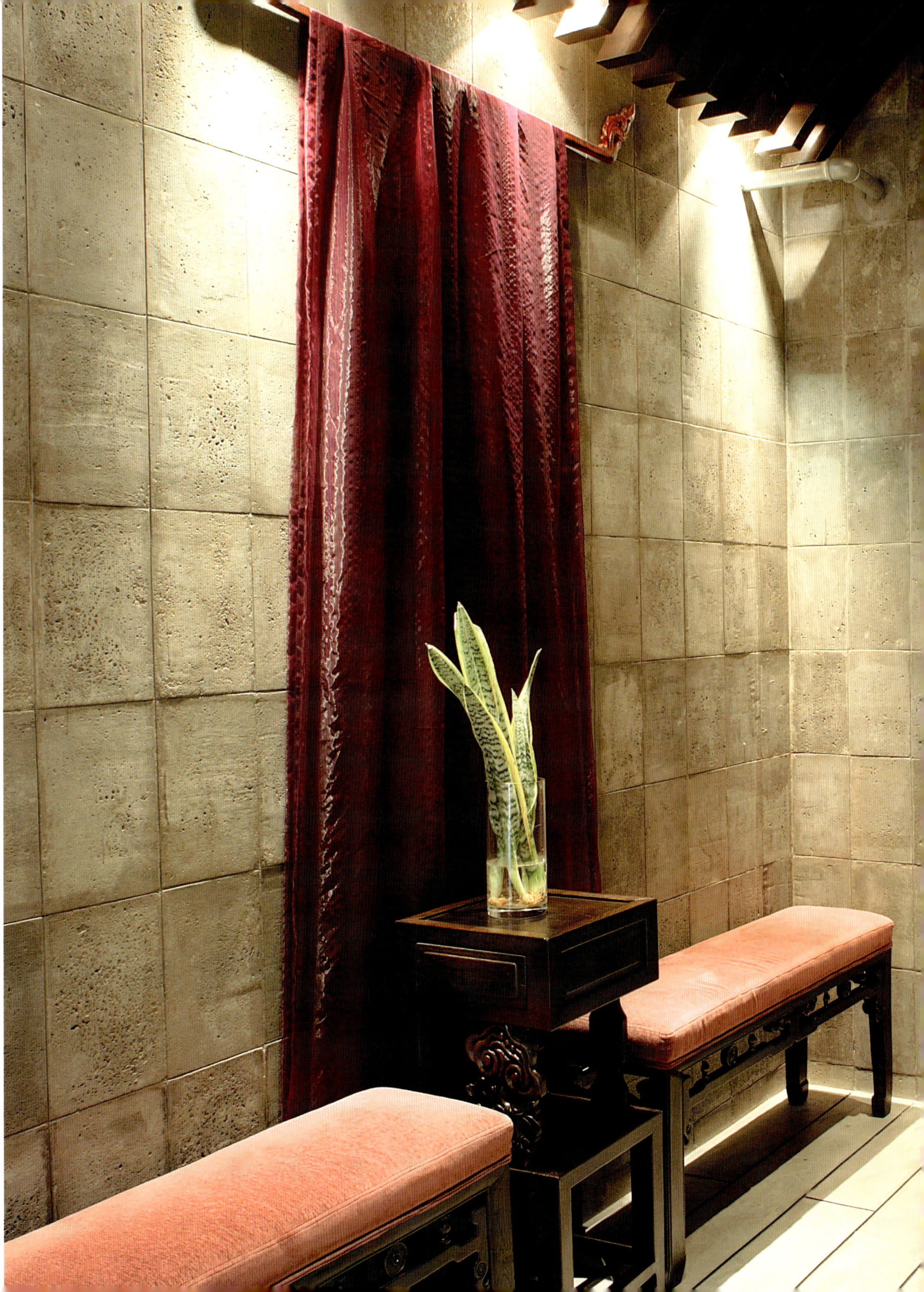

The soft furnishings in a room include carpets, heavy curtains, soft partition, louvres, cotton covers, beddings and cushions. In many cases, soft furnishings have fabric lining and they share one common feature-they can be changed any time in convenience. Soft furnishings in a space affects the overall colour appearance. Thoughtful homemakers will know that curtains should complement beddings and will keep two sets in line with season change, one for summer and the other for winter. Other types such as romantic, elegant, rich and simple beddings—in harmony with the ambience of a space—can enhance the home.

There are many types of soft furnishings. From a broader perspective, various synthetic woven materials can be used. However, they should be changeable. The wood microveneer, though known as woven material, is not a soft furnishing as it is fixed to surfaces and cannot be removed. Other materials such as soft covers for dadoes and fabric on ceilings are not considered soft furnishings too as they can neither be changed nor adjusted with colours.

Some materials, transparent or translucent in appearance, are soft furnishings. Gauze is often used with other materials. These sheer materials enhance the colours in a room. For example, a yellow covering placed against a blue curtain will give the curtain a touch of green. Change the yellow covering to red and the curtain appears violet. The matching of fabrics can greatly change the colour features in a room. Together with the use of techniques in space design such as the raising and lowering of curtains and the movement of furniture, the colours in the room will change and become more vivid to the eye.

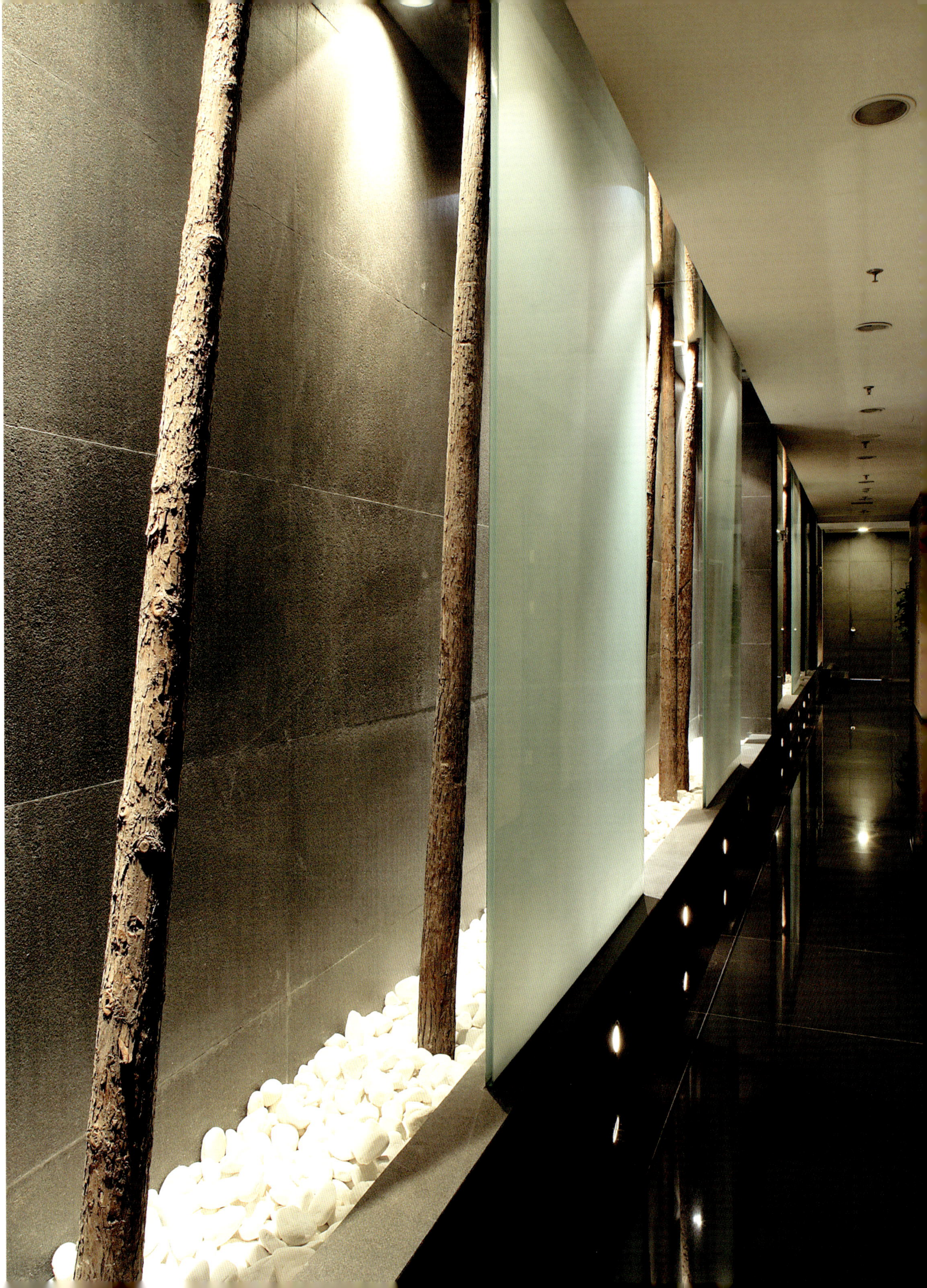

←
Neutral colours of low saturation give more highlight to the corridors.

A6 Colours and the Styles of a Room

In interior design, colours should not only meet the different functional requirements of a room but also create the aesthetic sense.

In practice, making an aesthetic and perceptual analysis of colours according to the functions of the room before designing is the key to an outstanding interior colour design.

Colours can express certain functions. For example, the use of different colours for construction areas will caution people of the danger in the vacinity.

←

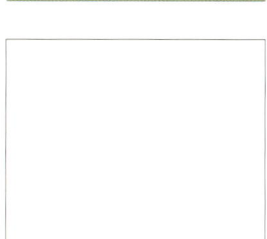

Interior Colour Design for Halls

Halls include hallways, aisled halls, entrance halls, elevator halls, waiting rooms and lobbies. These places have the highest flow of human traffic where many services are found. Hence, the interior design should express the function of the building and link with the other parts of the building. In view of this purpose, colours of low saturation are chosen as the main colours, accompanied by dense and eye-catching colours. For entrance and elevator halls which serve simple functions, accent colours used should complement the main colours.

→

Colours of low saturation are chosen as the main colour for corridors.

←

The pale yellow close to achromatisation provides a platform for furnishings.

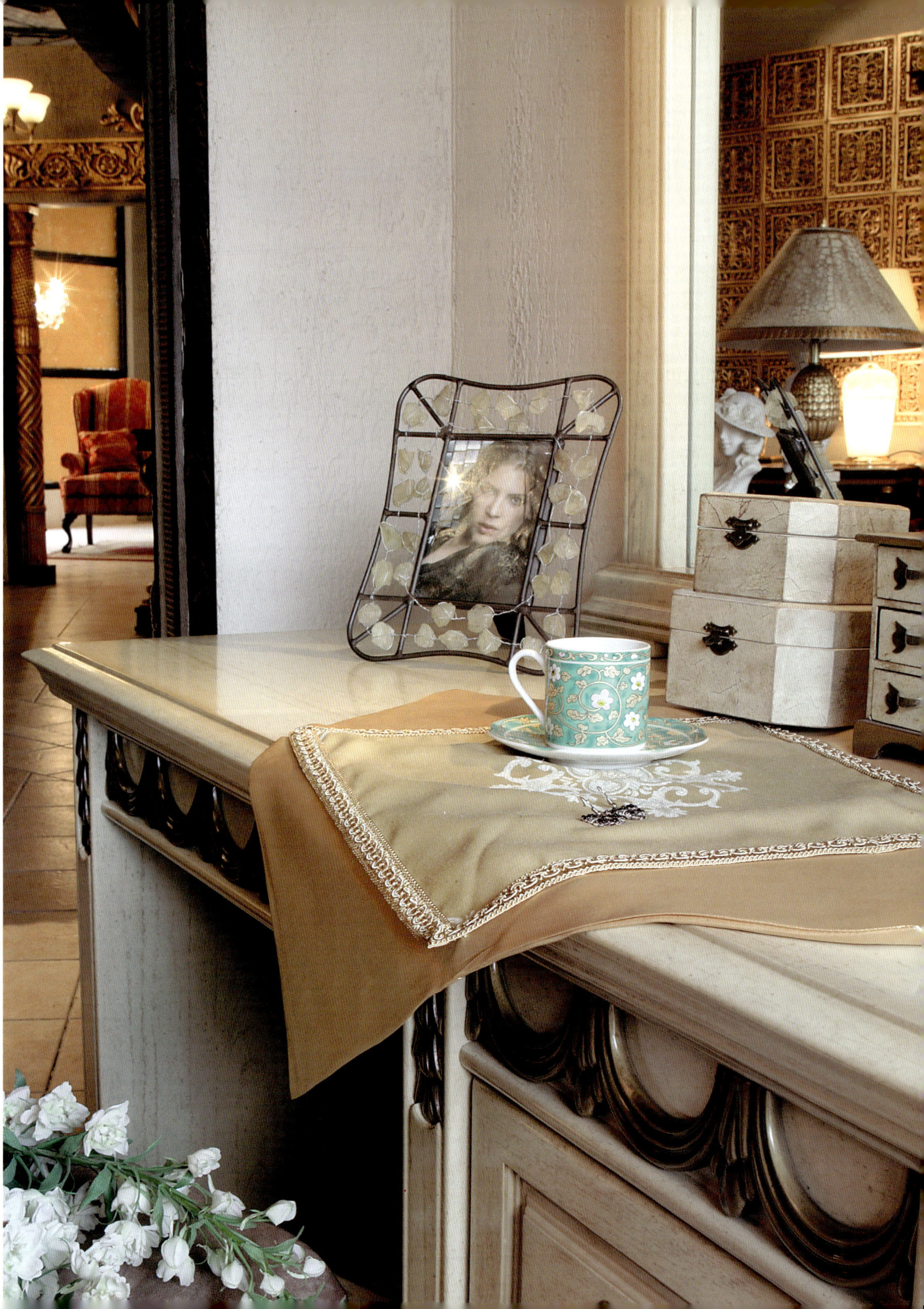

Interior Colour Design for Shops

Apart from the ceiling and floor, the interfaces in a shop are mostly hidden due to the many stalls and counters. The business hall displays goods so its interfaces should be in colours of low saturation and values, and the floors should be in neutrals to harmonise yet be distinguished from the cupboards and shelves.

←

To enhance the nostalgic ambience, the walls are painted in ropey white.

→
Achromatisation is a perfect setting for a dazzling array of articles.

←
The articles contend with the plain setting for appeal.

1.Boutiques

Boutiques are designed with customers' age and styles in mind. Most shops for fashionable teenagers are in bright and rich colours while branded boutiques for career women usually have achromatic colours and colours of low saturation as the accent colours with granite, fabrics or spot lights to express elegance.

Light colours are often chosen for women's clothing stores to contrast with the colours of the materials of the clothings.

For women's lingerie boutiques, shades of pink are often chosen to depict women's sensuality.

←
Warm colours show vibrance.

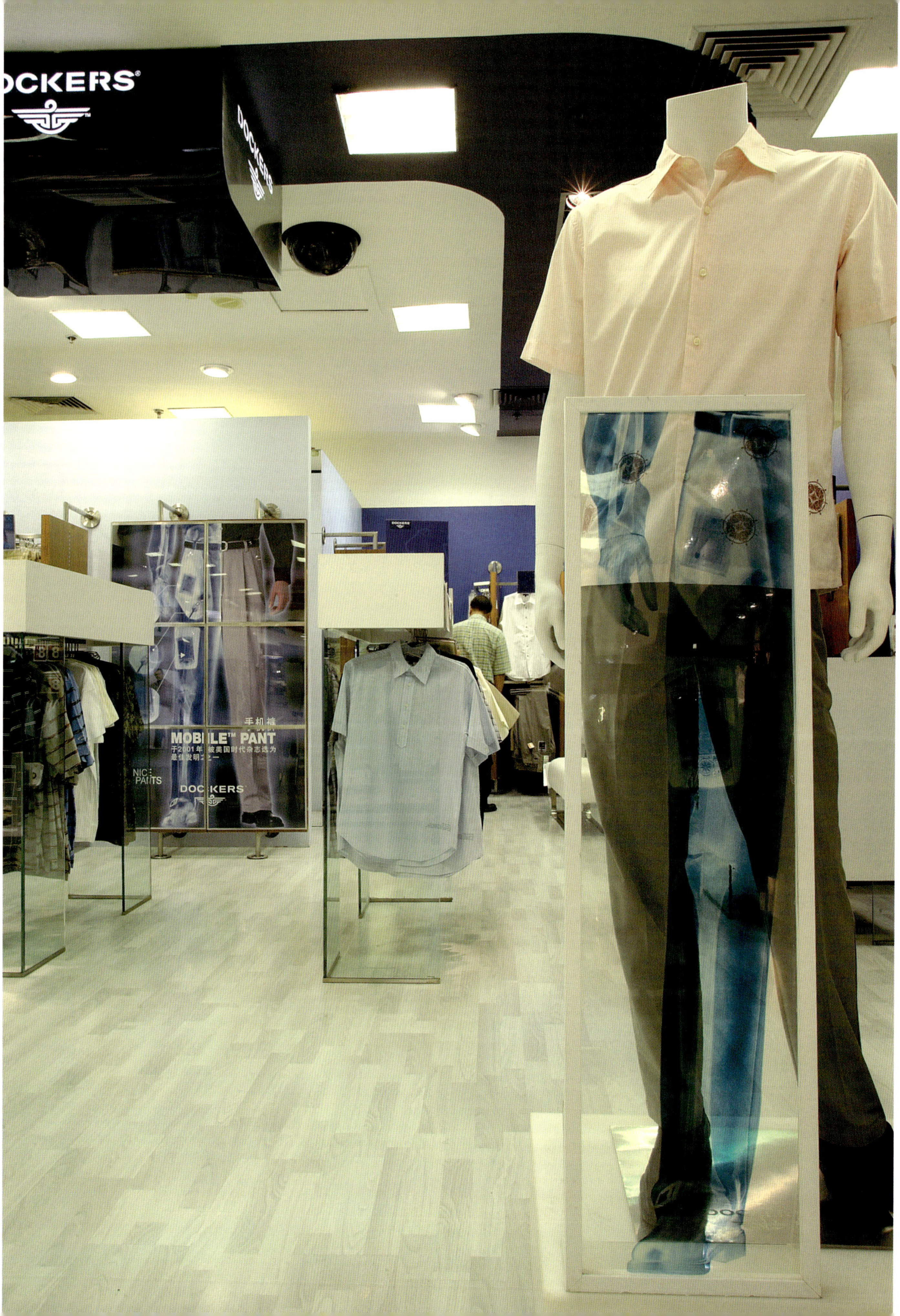
DOCKERS
手机裤
PANT
最佳发明之一
NIC
PANTS

Black portrays strength; glass expresses fortitude; and white harmonises everything in the space-a vernal masculine world.

2.Men's stores

Men's stores are often in achromatic colours, silver, brown and blue to depict men's masculinity and rationale. Hard materials such as stones and metals are also good choices. Recently, there has been a radical reformation in men's fashion which is accompanied by the changes in the design of men's stores. The age of chivalry is over. Many brightcolours such as flourescent green, heliotrope and even purplish pink define men's stores. However, men are still very much attached to black, a classic colour, and the colour is embraced to portray men's association with strength.

←
The black and white highlight the
jewellery individually.

3. Jewellers

Most jewellers display their goods in counters. Achromatic colours are chosen as accent colours while pure colours are chosen for counters to accentuate thegoods. Black or red velvet, or wood furnishings are often chosen for luxurious jewellery stores. Most traditional western styles adopt the black velvet while Chinese styles adopt the red velvet.

Jewellery business encompasses mostly negotiations. Thus, the stores often furnished as a showroom and the colour design is based on the style of the jewellery. Dark colours are generally chosen for classical jewellery. Together with fine pseudo classic furniture, these colours create a museum-like atmosphere. Colours for trendy fashion jewellery express various styles: primitive colours depict a return to nature, cool metallochrones associate with technology, and solid pure colours represent individualism.

←

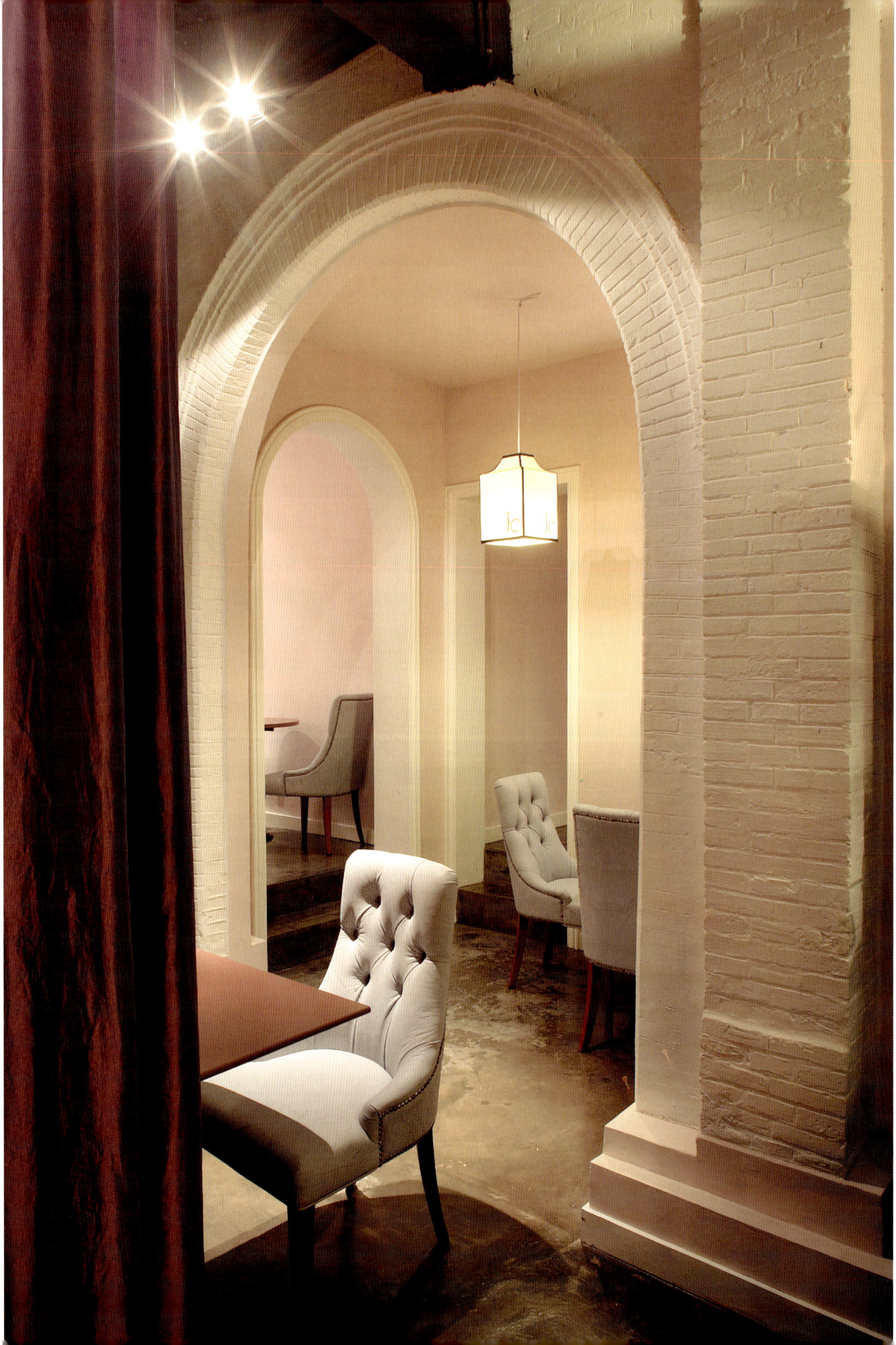

Interior Colour Design for Restaurants

←
The coffeebar has typical outdoor features but the delicate cream colour presents an indoor atmosphere.

↓
Cool colours are seldom used in Chinese restaurants but are more common in seafood restaurants.

Colours greatly affect people's appetite. Yellow, the most appetising colour, exudes a sweet fragrance. In contrast, food looks stale in blue-violet lights. This explains why most restaurants choose warm colours such as red, orange and yellow as their accent colours. White is a good colour scheme as it can match many other colours and is associated with cleanliness. Generally, restaurants should have warm lights and cool lights should never be shone directly on food.

Green, white and dark brown can be used for tea houses or bars to create a cool and refreshing environment while red-white or complementary colours can be used for fast food restaurants to accentuate simplicity. Banquet halls are usually in wood colours of low values with touches of red and silver to express luxury. Some seafood restaurants sometimes choose blue as their colour scheme but their tablecloths are mostly in white or warm colours.

Many coffee rooms have their own themes and colours are used to enhance that. Some dark bars can be lightened with the use of different lights to create a bizarre setting.

For most daytime restaurants—coffeebars not included—natural light and green plants are elements of the interior design.

←

←
Most Chinese restaurants choose warm colours.

→
Bright colours can be used in restaurants but white is more suitable for tabletops.

杨 建

旭 筑

←

This architectural company uses white to accentuate lights and shapes — two unique features used by the designers.

↙

White, the main colour, draws attention to the features in the space.

Interior colour design for educational institutions and offices

1. Interior colour designs for classrooms

The contrast between traditional blackboard and light-coloured walls increases students' visual fatigue. Many classrooms now have boards which are dark green. With a similar shade coloured wall which the board is set against and the other walls in light green, the effect is visually less taxing. Generally, colours of high values, low saturation and low reflection are chosen for the interfaces of classrooms to raise the level of illumination and promote homogeniety. In a classroom, there should be no more than three colours. Cool colours may be chosen for higher levels of learning as they have a soothing effect which will enhance the clarity of mind. For lower levels of learning, vibrant colours are encouraged.

2. Interior colour design for offices

The general rule of colour design for offices is that colours should clearly complement the functions of the building. Colours of low or medium values may be chosen as the accent colours for large office spaces while colours of medium or high values may be chosen.

Colours can also be used to define working areas, areas of large human traffic and meeting areas. Shades of low value grey are appropriate for working areas while vibrant harmonious colour schemes are suitable for areas of large human traffic. Meeting areas should be in colours of low or medium values to promote serenity.

Offices of senior management should be in colours that are soothing yet professional. Wood furnishings and cool colour schemes are the preferred choices. Metal and stone too exude elegance.

←

←

Interior Design for the Living Space

1. The living room

The living room is the window to the world beyond and the image of the family. Thus, it should reflect the host's characteristics: graceful, warm and friendly. Warm colours are commonly chosen to create a cozy atmosphere and often matched with wooden furniture and plants, and cool colours of low or medium hues for contrast.

2. The bedroom

People relax and sleep in the bedroom. Thus, a cozy, peaceful and soft atmosphere is needed. Colours of low saturation are the first choice. Colours of medium saturation or low to medium values are also ideal. However, raising the values of a dark room may greatly affect its atmosphere. Age also determines one's choice of colours. The young prefer colours of medium to high saturation to show the vibrance of their youth while bright and rich colours are chosen for childen's rooms to promote learning. For the elderly who prefer a sense of comfort, colours of low to medium values and saturations are chosen.

←

The drawing room is a 'new wineskin with old wine': the interfaces are modern while the colour and shapes of the furniture are traditional.

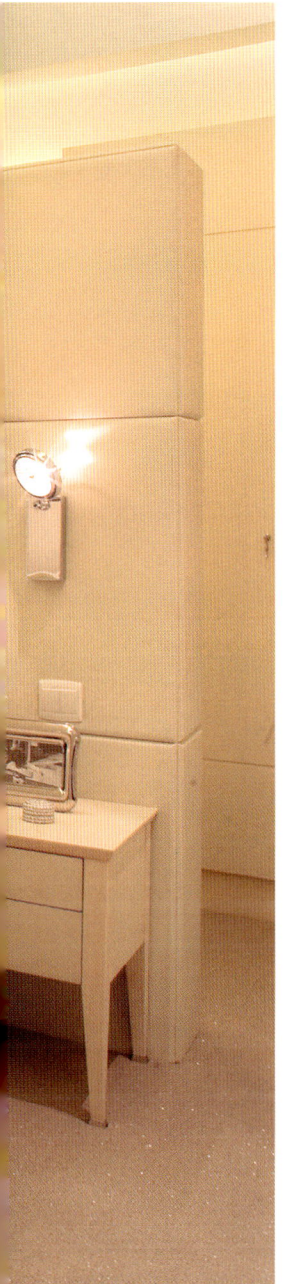

3. The dining room

The dining room can be designed with individualism in mind.

Cream, white and brown are classic colours for bedroom which transcend time.

Pale green and beige are appetising colours for areas in relation to food and beverage.

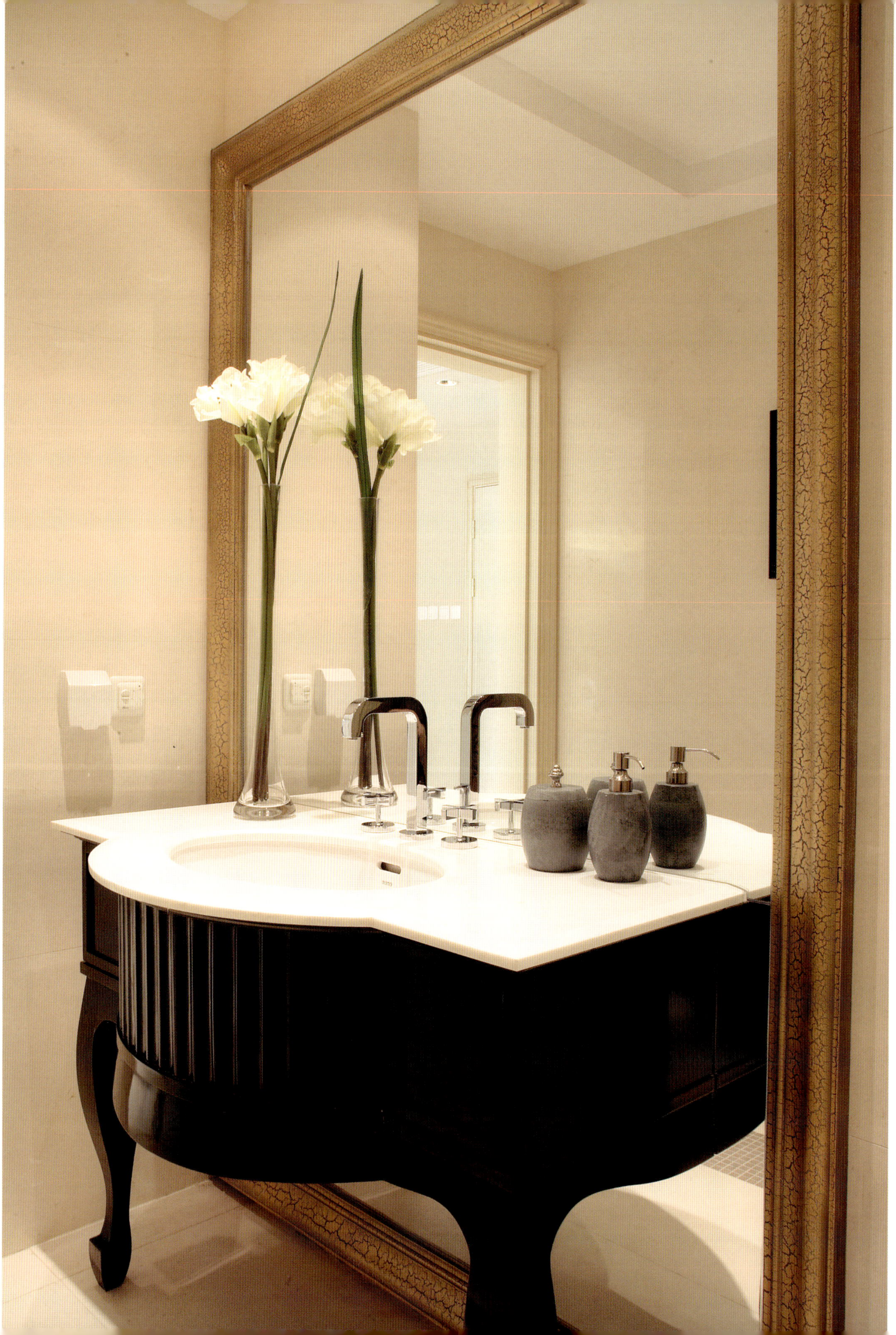

←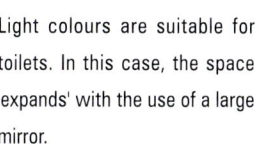

←
Light colours are suitable for toilets. In this case, the space 'expands' with the use of a large mirror.

4. Children's room

Children's rooms are often in pink while teenagers' rooms are in colours of high saturation or values. Bright vibrant colours are suitable for growing children.

5. Toilet

Many toilets are in white or light colours as they make the spaces look clean and tidy. This is especially true for small toilets because light colours 'enlarge' a space. The climate is another consideration: cool colours, with touches of neutral colours such as white and green, are used for toilets in tropical areas while warm colours and wood are used in toilets of temperate areas.

→

→
The pink tone of a child's room expresses parental care and a child's tenderness.

Interior Colour Palettes

Chapter Two:
The Expressions of Colours in Interior Design

Colours are not just the stimulation of light in the eyes but also a source of emotions. Certain colours stir certain emotions and thus, it is important to choose appropriate colours for particular rooms. Designers often choose colours based on age, occupation, characteristics and surroundings to create different atmospheres to meet certain needs of the occupants. Take the bedroom as an example. Pink and purple create a romantic ambience and are generally preferred by the young. For the middle aged, maroon is preferred. Blue, green and grey are suitable for wards in the hospitals as blue helps in regulating blood pressure and reducing the temperature, while green alleviates fatigue. Those living on the prairies adore red, the deserts green, and the clamourous cities light and soft colours. Differences and preferences in the choice of colours are mostly determined by the surroundings and lifestyle of occupants.

The ability to perceive and discriminate—through one's imagination and emotions—vary according to differences in hues. This variation is called 'the expression of colours'. Each hue has a different
expression, and this expression is fortified or altered when matched with different colours. Designers need to grasp this understanding to be able to use colours appropriately.

B1 Red and its Complementary Colours

Red symbolises flame, passion and revolt; it expresses terror, bloodshed and violence. A typical traditional Chinese colour and an indispensable colour in Chinese celebrations, red also symbolises happiness and good luck. The red pole is an important component of traditional Chinese construction. Red is used in many local patterns. North-eastern restaurants are usually laced with red-bottomed cotton prints. As red stimulates blood pressure and promotes blood circulation, it is the first choice of many fast food restaurants. Examples of Chinese and Western restaurants that make use of red are KFC, McDonalds, Yong He King, etc. It is believed that red whets appetites and therefore, increases consumption. American concerts which once adopted blue for their settings now choose red. According to colour researchers, red enhances audience's enjoyment of music.

←
Red appears different on different textile.

→

→
Red stands out in the absence of strong lighting.

↑
Red expresses passion and is a symbol of joyous celebrations.

→
The red yellow scheme expresses heat and passion while red against black brings about a sense of gloom.

← Pink is a symbol of tenderness.

Red Matching Pink

The matching of colours in the same series is harmonious. Pink reduces the strength of red and adds a touch of tenderness.

←

Warmer cool colours when matched with red, results in a reduction of the saturation of colours.

←

Red Matching Blue or Purple

Red is the warmest colour and should be handled with caution when matched with cool colours such as blue and purple. There are two precautions to take. The first is to choose a cooler red such as rose or purplish red to add a touch of warmth to blue and purple—an appropriate combination for pubs, dance halls and discos. Secondly, pink when matched with blue or purple, creates a harmonious and lively atmosphere. Pink is a light shade of red and is cooler in tone than red, yet brighter than blue or purple.

Red Matching Green

Red and green are complementary colours—colours of extreme contrast and the balance of the *yin* and *yang*. The same level of brightness highlights the contrast between the two colours and a poor match of them may bring about discomfort to a space. A way to avoid this is to reduce the purity of the two colours. The red and green used in Christmas designs is a classic match. This western style match is also adopted in living rooms or restaurants with Scottish square as patterns. Such a match is often used in western restaurants and only a handful of Chinese restaurants with country themes adopt it.

←

Green increases the saturation in red.

Red Matching Achromatic Colours

The netural nature of achromatic colours accentuates red as a resplendent colour and makes it the focus in a room.

B2 Orange and its Complementary Colours

Orange is an attractive colour and its passion is second to that of red, with the flame of red and the brightness of yellow. It symbolises life and is versatile. Orange is a good colour for foods, stimulating one's appetite. It exudes the aroma and sweetness of freshly baked bread. However, orange also has negative associations. It is the symbolic colour of Halloween, expressing jealousy and anxiety.

← Orange is an attractive colour.

Orange Matching Warm Colours

Orange Matching Blue

Orange embraces motion while blue stationary. These complementary colours show a contrast between motion and stationary and often appear in sports apparel. In many cases, a large space of blue is decorated with hints of orange to inject brightness and live.

←
Orange glows in warm colours.

→
Orange stands out in a space of blue.

Orange Matching Green

Orange and green complement each other. However, they also set off a contrast of warmth or cold. Both colours are full of vitality and life. They are often colours for fruit stores or dessert houses, and they are suitable for dining halls.

← Both colours are full of vitality and life.

→ Orange and green set off a dazzling contrast.

Orange Matching Black

This match is similar to colours of warning signs: attractive and resounding. When a large space of black is decorated with small areas of orange, a mysterious ambience is created. This explains why the two colours are chosen for Halloween: the orange pumpkins with black eyes grin in the day and the black pumpkins glitter orange from the eyeholes — a negative contrast of orange and black.

Black stands out attractively in a space of orange.

B3 Yellow and its Complementary Colours

Yellow is the colour of light, and is bright and stunning. It is a pure colour of the highest value which often associates with clarity, pleasure and speed. It is a symbol of wealth and prosperity as it is in the likeness of gold. In China, yellow represents royalty and power while in the West, yellow is associated with the dressing of Judas and thus, represents rebellion and jealousy.

Yellow appears weak and tender with white, and reserved with black.

↑
Yellow is the colour of light and
is enhanced by lights.

→

Golden yellow appears dazzling
in yellow light.

Yellow Matching Green

Yellow is the colour of buds, the prelude of green, and the beginning of life. This lively match reminds people of the greens, often associated with health and vitality. It can be used in cosmetic stores, food places and pharmacies. In China, green is the symbol of offspring and yellow is the symbol of early childhood.

← Yellow and green remind people of things such as plants and health.

Yellow Matching Warm Colours

Although yellow is a warm colour, it can still stand out in a space of warm colours because of its values. It gives off a sense of energy and when matched with warm colours, expresses individualism.

Yellow and red are arrogant colours and present a stark contrast when put together.

← Metallochrome alone is not strong enough to depict wealth and nobility; gold will shine brighter against a black or dark setting.

Yellow Matching Black

In most cases, black stands alone in yellow — rebelling like shadows in the blazing sun. Black against a yellow background becomes a warning colour. If yellow and black are matched appropriately, the yellow will be enhanced, just like the colour scheme of the emperor's robe in ancient China.

←

Green is an appropriate colour for the dining room.

B4

Green and its Complementary Colours

Green is the colour of most plants and it symbolises nature, vitality and growth. It is also the theme colour of peace and security. However, in the West, green symbolises evil and jealousy. It is also a colour chosen by educational institutions and libraries as it helps to reduce visual fatigue. To reduce surgeons' incidence of residual vision, greyish green is chosen for the walls of operating theatres.

↓

Green has much graduation and variation.

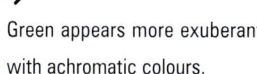

→
Green appears more exuberant with achromatic colours.

←
Yellowish green with orange stimulate the appetite.

Green Matching Achromatic Colours

↑

Green is the colour of life and appears exuberant against simple achromatic colours.

Green Matching Orange

←

Green is the colour of the stems of plants, and orange is the colour of fruits. The combination of the two colours offers the affluence and beauty of autumn, the pleasure of harvest, the aroma of delicious foods, and the warmth of a happy home.

Green Matching Neutral Colours

There are many secondary colours in nature and they are mostly associated with certain textiles such as bamboos, canes, linen, cotton, etc. Green is natural and is not confined even in the presence of secondary colours.

← Neutral colours such as linen, brown and grey are natural and comfortable — a good complement to green.

B5 Blue and its Complementary Colours

Blue is the colour of the sky and the sea, and also a symbol of the universe. It has a soothing effect, stimulating blood circulation and regulates pulse. Thus, it is often used in hospitals. Blue is also welcomed in tropical places as it bringsto mind the cool touch of water. Blue walls with white flooring and furniture is the classic colour scheme for seaside villas as the setting reminds people of the romance at sea. Blue is also used in ice cream parlours and seafood restaurants in view of its strong association with smells. In addition, the colour is also representative of intelligence and technology. In the West, blue symbolises nobility and royalty.

←

←

Blue brings to people the coolness of the night.

←
The purplish blue here balances
the warmth of the floor and the
bedroom appears calm.

Blue Matching Orange

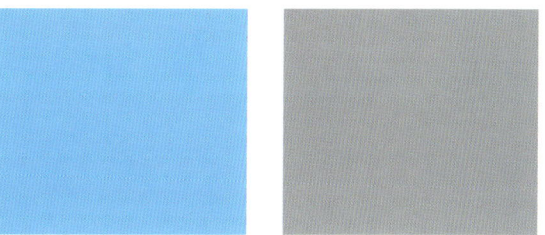 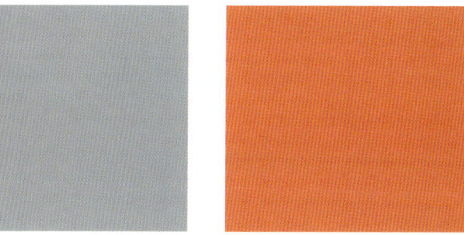

When blue dominates, the room feels cold. However, orange—a symbol of warmth—adds a different dimension to the room. In the presence of orange, blue represents expanse and space.

←
Adding orange to a space is like
lighting a lamp on a dark icy night.

Blue Matching Yellow

Blue, yellow and red are primary colours which strongly contrast with one another. When blue and yellow are matched, the contrast between the two colours are toned down.

↑

Adding blue to yellow tones down
the contrast between them.

→

Bluish-grey is the 'uniform' of
industrial places, representing
technology.

Blue Matching Turquoise

Blue appears in almost all interior spaces as the main theme. Technology is said to be represented by blue and is reflective of huge machinery and fast-running assembly lines. In this post-modernisation society, the advancement in technology has transcended the physical machinery to the intangible information highway. This is why flourescent green has replaced blue to represent the 'matrix'—an era of transition.

Purple and its Complementary Colours

As purple is the colour of traditional Chinese officials of the highest ranks and the colour of Greek kings, it is often associated with nobility and solemness. Purple is also associated with the night sky, the supernatural and mystery. Dark purple brings about a sense of depression, shame and arrogance. A pure shade of it symbolises mists and smoke, graceful, noble and illusive. Lavender is a feminine colour and is full of sweetness, charm, coyness and reticence.

←
Purple has a graceful, noble and
illusive feel.

Purple Matching Light Colours

Purple has a very low value and thus, it is easy to distinguish it from the other light colours.

←
Purple stands out in light colours.

Purple Matching Green

Purple matching green is a contrast of secondary colours, and the effect is less strong than that of primary colours. This is because the two colours harmonise better.

Purple Matching Warm Colours

Purple is a cool colour and adjustments to the saturation or value of warm colours should be made before putting them with purple.

→
When the value and saturation of warm colours are reduced, they become 'cooler' and can be easily matched with purple.

←
Purple and green give a rich contrast as they harmonise well.

↑
Black is the focus, accentuating
mystery, serenity and charm.

→
Black is a colour of strength.

→

B7 **Black and its Complementary Colours**

Black is the colour of the night, representing mystery, sorrow, solemness, silence and even death. It is a passive colour, absorbing lights but setting off other colours richly. In the West, it is the colour for funerals and formal occasions. Black is also a cool colour and gives a sense of infinite space. For example, when all the walls in a space are painted black, a sense of unity in the horizontal and vertical interfaces is created and the space appears to have no boundaries.

Black Matching Red

Black in red is a harmony of high values. Black, rebellious on one hand, is serene on the other in the presence of red.

←
Black enhances the richness and strength of red.

Black Matching White

Black and white are abstract, an ideal in colour harmonising. Both are neutral colours, contrast with each other, and are in perfect harmony. With a touch of bright colours, the space becomes lively.

← Black is a hard colour and harmonises with stones, glass, or square standing objects.

→ Adding red to the space, the black and white scheme becomes livelier.

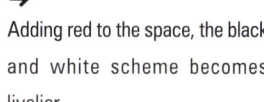

White and its Complementary Colours

Black and white are neutral colours. However, white is cooler than black as it reflects much light. Black is high in hue and is easy to match with. White is of great importance in a large space of pure colours; it lightens the intensity of colours. White is often neglected as a background because the pure colours, which are illuminated by white, draw greater attention. This can be seen in Chinese paintings and calligraphy where the characters and figures take the centrestage against the white backdrops. White symbolises purity, simplicity and holiness.

←
White shows the different depth
of grey in lights.

← White is the best setting for all
the other colours.

→

White is pure and innocent.

Black, White and Grey

Black, white and grey are neutral colours. Spaces and shapes are formed in their presence.

←

Here, white unifies the different
textiles, leaving only the veins in
their natural state.

B9 **Grey and its Complementary Colours**

Grey is the transition colour between black and white. It is rich in graduation and is a passive colour. It matches other colours well and when put next to red, grey will appear greenish — perfectly charming. Different shades of grey differ in values and saturations. Light grey appears weak, dark grey gives a sense of stagnancy, and middle-toned grey appears ordinary and dull. Grey is a good complementary colour and cause other colours to stand out.

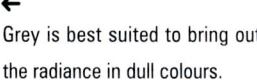

←

Grey is best suited to bring out the radiance in dull colours.

→

The grass green and the bluish grey, together with the red bricks, relate to the technological revolution in China.

Grey Matching Black and White

Grey, the transition colour between black and white, harmonises the two colours schematically.

←
Grey reduces the contrast
between black and white.

Grey Matching Bright Colors

Grey in a bright colour scheme is milder than achromatic bright colour scheme. The neutral of grey moderates the contrast of bright colours.

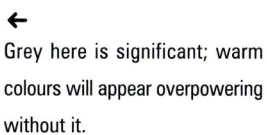

Grey here is significant; warm colours will appear overpowering without it.

Metallochrome and its Complementary Colours

Metallachrome in interior design includes gold, silver and various alloy colours. Gold and silver are the most commonly used. The Chinese love gold as it is the colour of wealth and nobility, and any posh Chinese or seafood restaurants will certainly carry it. The elegance of gold is very difficult to relay as it can easily be seen as obstrusive. Matching gold with black in Chinese calligraphy or painting creates a sense of wealth and solidity. Gold is warm and its appeal may be hindered by the presence of other pure colours. One way of preventing this is to use deep warm colours with gold, and use black to define them. Gold glows in cool colours, showing their cool metallic characteristics. Silver is a cool colour and gives greater sense of firmness when matched with other cool colours.

←
The metallic chain curtain has the strength of copper and evens out the contrast between red and green.

Metallochrome Matching Bright Colours

Metallochrome shows the grey characteristics when matched with bright colours. It is the best palette, creating various illusions with lights.

←
The window patterns, constructed with stainless steel and set against red panels, become attactive features in the room.

Metallochrome Matching Grey

Metallochrome is rich in saturation and on occasions, show hints of copper, gold and even turquoise.

←
Stained metals show hints of
yellow and green, and changes
with exposures to light.

Interior Colour Palettes

Chapter Three
Interior Colour Scheme

The following are three common approaches to planning interior colour schemes:

1.Interior Colour Scheme: Tone

In this scheme, two or more colours in harmony work to give visual pleasure. Colour experts established rules — according to the attributes of colours such as hue, value and saturation and their psychological effect on people — to determine colour schemes based on tone. A common approach is to use only one colour, in its various tints and shades. For example, for walls, shutters and carpets, analogous colours are used as the main colours, higher saturation analogous colours as the accent colours, and contrasting colours to the main colours as the colours to achieve certain moods.

2.Interior Colour Scheme: Contrast

Like colour schemes based on tone, this scheme too has established rules. However, the rules serve not for the purpose of harmony but for contrast. For example, a hue is chosen as the main colour and its value and saturation are adjusted for the main interfaces while colours contrasting to the main colours are used as the accent colours-used to achieve certain moods.

3.Interior Colour Scheme: Style

This scheme has been adopted by some popular styles in history and currently, it is used to create certain moods and associations. Designers, in using this scheme, must not only have a rich knowledge of colours and design but also understand the cultural background of their audience who are to read, interpret and appreciate the work.

C1 Interior Colour Scheme: Tone

Tint

Tint is an elegant tone. The light pastels of a tint create soft and gentle environments. The softness brings to mind smooth complexions and the tenderness of babies and often, such colours are used in rooms of infants. However, even in such a use, different colours establishes different associations: pastel yellow as a symbol of warmth and life; pastel blue as a symbol of serenity and solitude; pastel purple as a symbol of mystery and illusiveness; pastel green as the symbol of nature and imminent spring; and finally, pastel orange as a symbol of hope and sweetness. These associations help determine the use of colours in certain areas like cosmetics and linen. Take cosmetics as an example. Pastel green is suitable to depict innocence, pastel purple to depict elegance, and pastel yellow to depict warmth.

Elegance is communicated by the purity of pastels.

The use of tint does not necessarily mean that the colours in a room are only limited to pastels. Often, pastels are the main colours while colours of a lower saturation of the pastels are the accent colours and colours with low values are the colours used to achieve certain ambiences.

Generally, the tint is suitable for creating spaces in which people spend long hours. In such a use, complementary colours are more appropriate. An example is a ladies' spa which has contrasting cool and warm colours—an expression of women's rich emotions.

Pastel yellow is the strongest among the pastels, as the other pastels of a high saturation have only medium values. On the other side of this spectrum is white. It is best loved by designers who adopt the minimalist style where beauty lies in the absence of colour.

←
Add some colours of lower saturation to the pastels.

←

↓

→

Pastels create a comfortable and relaxed atmosphere.

←

Pastel yellow is the only pastel that has a high value.

↓
Dark colours blend into the dark-coloured setting while light colours distinguish themselves from it.

The Shade

The shade gives a sense of heaviness and gloom, but it is the coolest colour. When you walk into castles of the Middle Ages, you will witness the charm of shades: the cold rock walls, dark stairs, heavy curtains and elaborately engraved ornaments. The shades are further enhanced by the weak lighting in the room, and the dark colours symbolise wealth and luxury. It is commonly believed that light colours are for the ignorant, grey for the working class, and dark colours for the nobles. This is reflected in Chinese dwellings. There is nothing more than white walls, grey tiles and wood furniture for the common public while high officials and nobles have dark-coloured classic furnishings and padauk furniture.

Some modern spaces also use the shade. In the movie *The Matrix*, two colours represent the future: pure black and pure white. The black and white spaces show a complete absorption of lights and a complete reflection of lights respectively. Thus, the spaces have no sense direction and an illusionary future is created. In most cases, white is seldom used to create an illusionary future as it may appear grey in a setting of different values. On the other hand, a dark room gives a sense of endless boundaries where the interfaces integrate as one. This nature of pure black carries with it a strong sense of individualism, something particularly welcomed by the rebellious young.

In the colour schemes for shades, while colours of medium values may be chosen to enhance a space, there is no colour which is stronger than black.

The dark tone is suitable for use with lights. In Yang Huishan's glace workshop, the dark tone draws attention to her works by means of dim lights. This use of dark tones and lights can be seen in museums and art galleries.

←

The colours in the club are fused by dark colours.

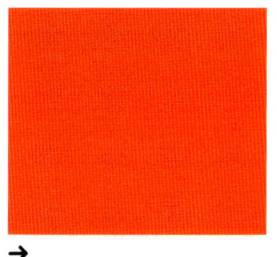

→

Dark colours are suitable for bars and lounges.

← The cool shades bring out the richness of the colours.

→ Through the manipulation of lights, variation of the deep colours is produced.

The Vibrant Tone

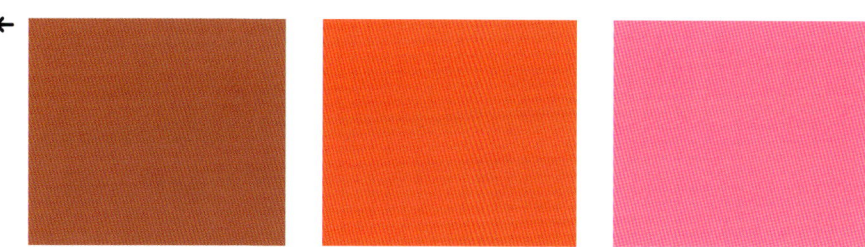

The bright colour scheme is visually dramatic. High saturation not only brings attention to the colours, it also shows the individualism of the colours. Not all hues give a bright tone. In both well-lit and dark areas, most colours cannot be of a high saturation because of their values. Thus, besides pure yellow or purple, there are no colours which can form a bright tone. The bright tone refers to the different colours of medium saturation, including red, green, orange, blue and their secondary colours.

←

Almost all bright colours have the highest saturation with medium values.

→
Bright colours should not be matched with more than two colours.

The bright colour scheme is suitable for commercial spaces. As people do not spend long hours in such spaces, the bright tone will leave a deeper impression. It can also stimulate one's appetite. Some examples include the red in *KFC*, the yellow and red in *McDonald's*, the orange in *Kodak*, the green in *Fuji Film*, etc. Red is the most common in fast food restaurants. It not only whets the appetite, it also tires people out easily because of its strong values.

←
The black structure of the divider strengthens the brightness of the red and gold.

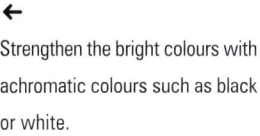

← Strengthen the bright colours with achromatic colours such as black or white.

→ The room looks less empty with the use of bright-coloured furnishings.

The bright colour scheme usually comprises one hue as the key colour and the rest of the achromatic colours as complementary colours. A monochromatic colour scheme is simple to manage. When a bright colour scheme is combined with other colour schemes, the relationship between them becomes more complex. For example, a red colour scheme, when introduced to other colour schemes, affects the overall appearance of the space. Generally, matching red with warm colours strengthens the red and intensifies the warmth produced by the other colours. One should be cautious when matching red with cool colours: purple should go with blue; dark green with green; and purple with red.

←

The Sombre Tone

Grey is most favoured by modern designers. Concrete, stainless steel and flagstones—natural grey materials. Why the grey tone? Modernists believe that only dull colours in the absence of furnishings can show the true beauty of the space and best serve the functionality. Rough surfaces of bare concrete and holes are left untreated. In Tadao Andro's theory, the first thing the eye comes into contact with is plain concrete wall. The same goes for the interior-natural coloured floor showing light veins, huge French windows in steel frames and glass panes, and furniture of grey cotton and wood. The entire created space is unadorned and spacious. "Let the space speak for itself," Modernists say. People are welcomed to discover the beauty of a building without ostentatious influences—a typical modernistic style.

Warm and cool colours blend into a space easily when the saturation is reduced.

← The grey tone, expressed in concrete, is representative of the relationship between humanity and history.

The space in a room of grey tone must be very rich in shapes, graduation and shadow effects to allow for greater visibility of designers' touch. For such spaces, it is better set in a natural environment of lush greenery or scenic surroundings. The beauty of nature will become the centrepiece of attention against the simple and plain setting.

The grey tone can define objects well in commercial spaces. For example, in clothing boutiques and art galleries, the grey tone brings out the richness of objects in the spaces and prevents unnecessary clashes of colours.

→ The grey setting does not draw attention away from the objects in the space.

A room in grey tone enhances the visibility of the natural veins of materials used. Although the objects in the space are of the same colour, the different textures and treatments of the materials bring differentiation in the presence of light-rough, smooth, dark and loose, all of which are called 'the art of vision'.

It is not advisable to have large areas of pure colours for touch. Green plants or natural wood are recommended. Raising the contrast of values and adjusting the graduation of a space will help reduce monotony.

The lights bring individuality to the grey shades.

The Cool Tone

The cool colour scheme signifies rationalism. Blue is the coolest hue and second to it is purple. Cool colours bring relaxation, regulate the pulse, reduce blood pressure, and calm. In some hospitals, cool colours are chosen for wards of patients running temperature and the effect of the colours apparently works! Cool colours are associated with the cold, clarity and spaciousness. The very mention of summer houses reminds people of seaside villas, in a setting of blue waves and white sand, and blue walls and white floors. The blue and white scheme is popular for its association with the tropical scene.

I remember the time I went to my childhood friends' houses. The walls were in either pastel blue or green. I had believed it was to create an environment friendly to our eyes but I now know it was to make the place more spacious. This is referred to as the 'sense of expansion and recession'. It is the play of perception at work. Cool colours help 'steal' more room for a space. On the contrary, if a room is very large and is sparsely furnished, cool colours will make the place dull. In this case, warm colours are better used.

Cool colours are best matched with metallochrome. Metallochrome glitters with faint coolness in the presence of cool colours. If the values of the cool colours are reduced to contrast with the values of metallochrome, the metallochrome will stand out more.

←
The plants are full of vitality in the cool tone.

←
Colours and textures should be
skilfully handled in a design where
the cool tone is used.

Warm colours become cooler when white is added. An example is red. When white is added to it, the red turns pink. Pink is slightly purplish and brings across a sense of sadness when matched with yellow or pale orange. However, when matched with blue or green, it appears modest and assumes the liveliness of flowers in spring, bringing life to the cold surroundings.

Cool colours are in great harmony with natural scenery. The greens, turqoise and blues are natural colours of the sky and sea. That is why natural scenery matches well with cool colours. Unlike warm colours, cool colours are less dramatic and more sympathetic.

→
Blue is less monotonous in the
presence of white.

The Warm Tone

As the name suggests, warm colours produce warmth. Red, orange, yellow and their like are warm colours. These colours excite and stimulate heartbeat and blood pressure. As most objects associated with heat are of these colours, they create a warm feeling in the minds of people. All associations of warm colours are mostly emotion related: passion, stimulus, impulsion, celebration, happiness, etc.

People living in temperate countries love the warmth. Experiments show that the temperature of people can go up or down between three to four degree Celsius in a room of warm or cool colours. In cool areas, you may see red brick walls, maroon feathers and various heavy dark-coloured fabrics.

The warm tone is also common in Chinese restaurants. It makes the hot food more appetitising and creates a warm setting for gathering of family and friends. Warm colours are prevalent in happy events in one's life: marriage, child birth, promotion and even funerals. The Chinese are so attached to red that it is the national colour. In contrasts, there are more cool colours such as green and blue in western restaurants.

The warm colour scheme is intensified by lights.

Warm colours make a room 'fuller' and more colourful with a stronger sense of furnishing. This use of warm colours is called the 'economical technique'. Warm colours also brighten a dark room. Many believe that light colours brighten a space. Little do they know that warm colours are more effective in doing so as they add a sense of colouration.

Besides the warm and cool colour scheme, the achromatic and warm colour scheme is also a good match. To exemplify this, when one eats in excess foods of the same taste, eating foods of other tastes will restore the sensitivity of the taste bud and hence, enhance the eating experience. The achromatic and warm colour scheme works in the same fashion.

←

Yellow, orange, red and brown work to create a warm environment.

→

Contrast of values adds graduation to the warm tone and prevents monotony.

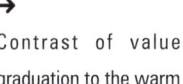

→
Cool colours regulate the warm tone.

Warm lights increase the saturation of warm colours.

The Achromatic Colour

In an achromatic colour scheme, there are only black, white and shades of grey. The common approach of this scheme is: white as the main colour and occupies the greatest space; black as the accent colour and its tertiary colours of low saturation as colours for touch; and shades of grey as secondary colours. As achromatic colours may at times be monotonous, varying the values would liven its total appearance.

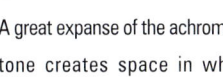

A great expanse of the achromatic tone creates space in which myriads of stories can be told.

White as the main colour gives graduation under various lights.

Different types of grey are used
in the achromatic tone: warm,
cool and neutral.

The achromatic colour scheme is representative of an ideal space in the natural world: there is great allowance for artificial expressions. I remember having once seen a speciality store—which sells suits and tuxedos-in achromatic colour. The achromatic colour scheme is an extension of the Metropolitan setting, and the black suits and tuxedos contrasts fittingly with it.

This colour scheme is also rampant in large public spaces such as offices, exhibition halls, hotels, etc. It accentuates the broad and grand buildings and establishes a plain setting in for them in which other furnishings can be easily accommodated.

There are two ways in which colour can be added to the achromatic scheme. One way is to add a larger space of colours of low saturation. The colours should be in harmony, for example pastel blue and pastel purple. The second way is to add a smaller space of pure colours. Potted plants or flowers may be added to a space of achromatic colour scheme, but take care to not affect the overall simple style depicted by the colour scheme.

Touches of colour in the setting
of white accentuates the elegance
of the achromatic colour scheme.

C2 **Interior Colour Scheme: Contrast**

The Contrast of Values

The contrast of values sets a clear contrast of black and white which works very well in most Chinese designs — dark furniture stand out against white walls. The furniture in Chinese designs are mostly wooden: table legs, footstools and the framework of the furniture form strong dark lines against the white setting. The charm is parallel to that of Chinese calligraphy. In the Neo-Chinese style, dark floors are replaced by white bricks and paintings on the walls are replaced by abstract ones. The furniture in the Ming Dynasty differ from that in the Qing Dynasty, turning from an elaborate style to a concise style.

Clarity and simplicity are the merits of contrast of hues.

←
The narrow corridor appears more spacious when the saturation of the ceiling and floor are reduced.

The contrast of values best expresses the spaciousness and graduation of a room. The shapes of the objects stand distinct in space of contrasting values. However, in light of this, black appears to be receding while white, advancing. This visual effect affects the overall expression of the room.

→
The foreground is distinct when a deep colour is chosen as the main colour.

The graduation of the accent and main colour stand out in the contrast of values.

The key of the contrast of values is to vary the saturation. Generally, there should be black and white in any colour design, with one as the main colour and occupying a larger space. In a classic case of contrast of values, white is chosen as the main colour with large interfaces of the space and furniture in that colour. White, under different lightings, shows shades of colours or grey in different objects. In contrast, black absorbs light and creates less shades of grey, making the space dull and empty. In a large space of white, use black for larger objects such as furniture, carpet or main wall. They may be in one colour, black, or in black and white patterns. The introduction of black to a space sets a strong contrast to white and hence, creates a visual impact on the eyes.

Other colours, even pure colours, may be added to the contrast of values. As black and white has the strongest contrast, it does not matter if the other colours occupy relatively smaller spaces.

The Contrast of Saturation

The contrast of saturation is formed by the juxtaposition of light and dark values and their relative saturation. There are three types:

1. Monochromatic and grey contrast

This scheme shows strong and single-colour features such as red matched with maroon or pink. The theme of this colour scheme plays on the expression of colours and gives a very strong colour sense.

2. Bright and achromatic colours contrast

In this scheme, achromatic colours are the main colours while bright colours are the accent colours, usually used for walls. The same colour, usually in small objects, is often used for touch.

↑

The touch of red brings joy to the dark room.

→

Bright colours are even brighter against achromatic colours, and black further strengthens them.

3. Bright colours and different hues of low saturation contrast

In this scheme, red may be used as the key colour in a large space of high saturation while green as the secondary colour, occupying a smaller space and of a lower saturation. The effect is interesting: red becomes even brighter as the colouration increases against green.

The three types of contrast of saturation have their distinct features: the achromatic and grey contrast is harmonious; the bright and achromatic colours contrast is simple, practical and effective; and finally, the bright colours and different hues of low saturation contrast is striking and hence, requires the designers to have a good knowledge of the proportion and density of the colour scheme.

The crux in the contrast of grey and bright colours is the proportion of the latter. Generally, for a place where people spend long hours in, bright colours occupying great spaces is not advisable as visual fatigue may set in. On the contrary, in places where there is heavy traffic, a large space of bright colours will create a visual centre stage where most attention is drawn. This technique is often adopted for entrance halls, aisles and traffic spaces of public buildings.

The bright colours and grey
establish a strong contrast.

←
Soft furnishings brighten the grey setting.

→
The bright colours add a touch of flamboyancy to the simple grey colour scheme.

The Contrast of Warm and Cool

The warm and cool colour scheme has the best colouration effect. According to colour experts, this colour scheme gives a balanced visual sense that is pleasing to the eye. The human eyes first distinguish the cool colours from the warm ones, and then put them together in a full colour spectrum that is both complimenting and harmonious.

← The contrast of warm and cool colours make them appear warmer and brighter respectively.

→ Warmth comes from the red while the texture of glass and iron gives a sense of cool.

The contrast of warm and cool colours creates an interesting spatial effect. As cool colours 'recede' and white 'advances', using the two on the same surface will create a three-dimensional effect of rich graduation. At the same time, as warm colours 'expand' and cool colours 'contract', the sense of space is further altered, adding more charm to the contrast of warm and cool colours.

← →
Unifying warm and cool colours
of the same values requires skill.

The contrast of warm and cool colours is suitable for many kinds of places: dining halls, hotels, entertainment arenas and residential houses. This colour scheme shows a rich contrast and is appropriate for long-time stay and appreciation. Dining halls, which adopt the warm and cool colours contrast, lend themselves a formal appearance.

The contrast of warm and cool colours is suitable for colours of average values as the colours harmonise well. Any other light colours of high values — besides yellow — will affect the overall effect: the warm colours will turn cool and the cool colours will turn warm. Similarly, the nature of the dark colours of low values will also change.

←
Cool and warm colours remain distinct in the same space.

The Contrast of Complements

Complementary colours are the colour wheel or perceptual opposites. When two complementary colours combine, dark grey will be produced. Complementary colours create a sense of colour balance in the human brain and thus, the eye can see the whole image clearly. This process is called 'the biological balance of vision'. In this, the contrast of complementary colours will appear stronger.

Compared with other kinds of contrast, this contrast is the strongest and the effect, fuller and more vibrant. In view of the balance of vision, the complementary colours share a relationship that is both in conflict and harmony. An inappropriate match may result in the complementary colours coming into complete conflict. Here are some techniques for harmony:

1. Use a hue as the accent colour, raise its saturation, and use it on the larger objects. Reduce the saturation of its complementary colour and use it as a secondary colour.

2. Apply one or two complementary colours in low saturation to a large space and colours of high saturation to a smaller space as the focal point.

3. When two colours are bright, put them with achromatic colours. This will raise their saturation and colouration. This technique is widely used, particularly for Middle Ages churches where stained glass are cast in iron.

Red is the main tone and green reduces the saturation.

4. Integrate the two complementary colours. For example, put a small space of green in red and vice versa. This technique creates a strong yet subtle contrast.

There are three common schemes for the contrast of complementary colours: the red-green scheme, the blue-orange scheme, and the yellow-purple scheme. As red and green have the strongest saturation of average values, the contrast is not affected by the contrast of values and is thus pure and bright. The contrast of blue and orange has the strongest sense of warmth and cool while the contrast of yellow and purple is weak because the contrast of values is stronger than that of hues.

Among the colours of low saturation, green and red compete with each other for attention.

Interior Colour Scheme: Style

We are fortunate to be living at a time whereby different styles and their functions are accepted. Through modelling, colour designing, selection of materials, and the arrangement of layout of interfaces, furniture and furnishings, a style is birthed and this sets the design apart from the rest.

The styles of interior colour scheme are mainly divided into two categories: eastern and western. The eastern styles include the traditional style of Ming and Qing Dynasty, the Japanese Meiji style, and the Muslin style in Southeast Asia. The western styles include the Roman style, the Gothic style in early Europe, the Baroque and Rococo style of the Middle Ages, and the Neo-classicist, Modernist and Post-Modernist styles of the 19th century. The current styles in China are: the modern concise style, the Neo-Chinese style, the western classical style, the natural style, the elegant style, the vanguard style, and the combination style.

The modern concise style is commonly adopted.

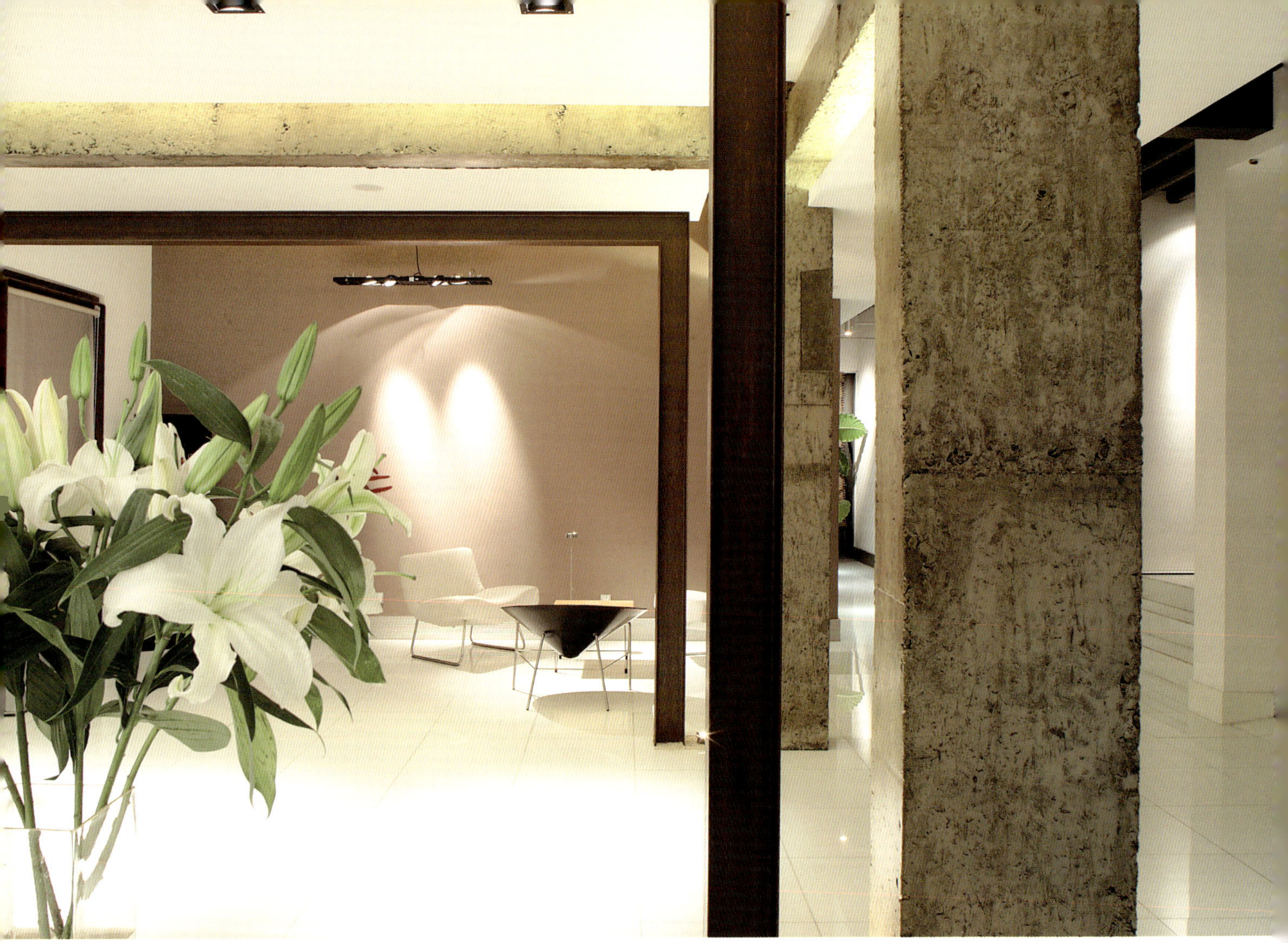

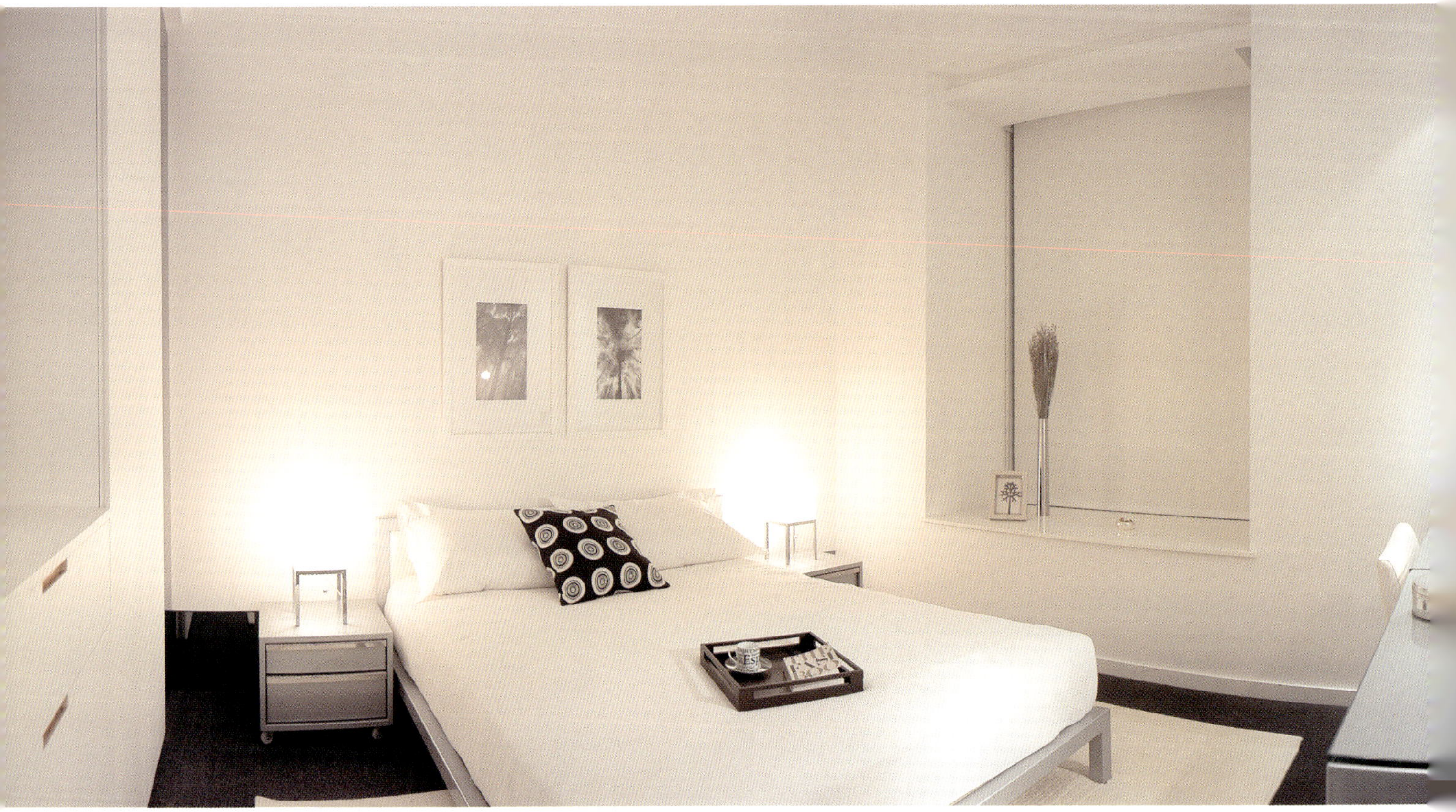

The Modern Concise Style

← The modern concise style includes the exposure of structures in the space, unlike the traditional concise style that pursues perfection.

The popularity of modern concise style in interior design in China has climbed since 2001. Some say the style stems from Modernism as it shares the same philosophy as Modernist, Miss Van Delo's "less is more". Others say it is near to the White style as it embraces the use the plain colours. There are also some who say that it is an extension of Functionism as it emphasises function and practically. In the modern concise style, white is the main colour and the interior of the space is simple and definite. However, beyond the treatment of surfaces with white, this style seeks to integrate the outside with the interior space: we see the scenery outside the room through the windows. Using this method of 'borrowing the scene', designers highlight the rich and colourful scenery outside through the plainness and clarity inside. In addition, the modern concise style makes full use of the beauty of variation of materials and space.

← The modern concise style is about simplicity and clarity.

The Neo-Chinese Style

The Neo-Chinese style adopted and added to the classical elements of the interior styles of the Tang and Qin Dynasty. It does not follow the original conception of layout but uses the modern arrangement of spaces. The colours used in this style are distinct and serious, and furnishings are sparse—all of which add to the unique charm of the Neo-Chinese style. The furniture used are mostly padauk, and matched with white walls or black tiles. Some designs make use of the colour scheme of Suzhou Gardens: white walls, black tiles, grey rock features, red poles, green trees and bamboos, clear water, and blue sky. Other designs make use of western style colour scheme where contrast of values is emphasised: white ceilings and walls, and dark-coloured furniture. The Neo-Chinese style has become a popular icon in the field of design in China, particularly favoured by the rich, academics and artists.

←

The Neo-Chinese style does not only replicate the classics; it emphasises the structures of furniture and the black and white contrast in Chinese paintings.

Like a new dress, the charm of Neo-Chinese style comes not from the material but the artistic essence of it.

←

The space appears traditional, but the modern style is embedded in the treatment of the walls and ceiling.

The Western Classical Style

The vocabulary of the Western classical style is rich: the resplendent Baroque, the aesthetical Rococo, and the indifferent Roman style. The classical style is rich and elaborate, and welcomed by the urban rich. The colours used are mostly magnificent and grand: yellow, orange and gold reflect wealth; maroon wood veins depict elegance; white granite expresses spendour; and gold and silver threads show strength. In addition, the dark colour scheme is representative of the Western classical style: dark blue and green wall paper, harvest-patterned heavy curtains and detailed dark carpets form a picture of nobility.

This style is suitable for large spaces to create a sense of presence and not small ones.

←

The Western classical style is suitable for high-ceiling and spacious rooms.

→

Other elements are added to this western classical design: glass screen Chinese calligraphy and modern brick floors.

←

↑

←

The ceiling of classical western architecture is heavy and elaborate.

The Natural Style

The natural style abandons complication and luxury. Instead, it emphasises comfort and liberty and advocates a 'return to nature'. This style is relaxed and comfortable. Bulky furniture, nostalgic ornaments, log floors, simple yet elegant bamboo curtains, and cotton floral table cloths — they all create a pleasant space. The colours for the natural style are mostly earth colours with green and brown being the most common. Wallpapers are pure paper pulp with floral design prints, just like the prints on the curtains. In some natural style designs, earth and nostalgic colours with rich fragrance of the soil are the first choice for walls.

The uncovered purlin, rough metope, plain wood window blinds and the empty cage remind us of life in the village.

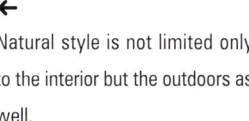
Natural style is not limited only to the interior but the outdoors as well.

← White is used to complement the earth ware.

The Elegant Style

The elegant style is birthed at the turn of the century. It has the romance of European Classicism and the depth of Modernism. It reflects the exquisite of life. This style has the modern style layout but is closer to classicism in aesthetics. The elegant style emphasises proportion and the harmony of colours, where there are no strong contrast and gaudy colour schemes. Much attention is paid to the harmony of colours when choosing materials. The wallpaper is a major furnishing textile and is often the main or accent colour. It has fine and elegant veins and matched with cotton in the same patterns.

←
Delicate veins and patterns are found in a space of elegant style.

←

Wood carvings of flowers and weeds
on the doors and windows express the
delicate female emotions.

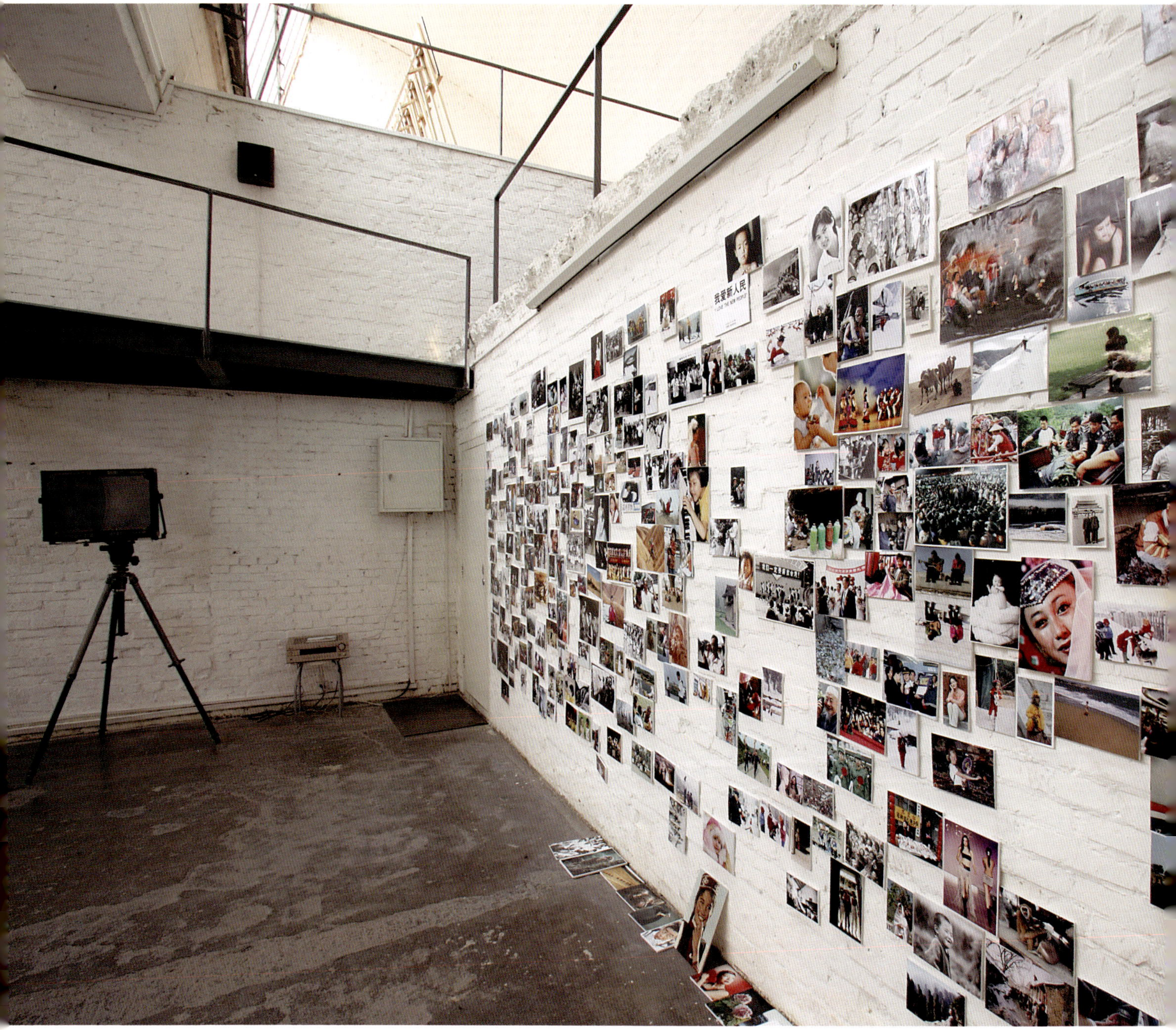
我爱新人民
I LOVE THE NEW PEOPLE

↑

The Vanguard Style

With the turn of the century, the vanguard style — known to oppose traditional aesthetic ideas — rose in popularity in the field of design. It advocates individualism and self-expression, reconstruction of spaces, the use of bright colours that give strong contrast, and unconventional choice of materials. There are many approaches to in the practise of the vanguard style: some use only one colour; some use colours of different saturation for several large spaces to make a statement; some use only black to create a space without the sense of interfaces and vectors; and some select unconventional materials to create visual-tactile conflicts that would draw attention.

↑

Create an uncommon setting with uncommon colours, giving an unconventional appearance.

→

Modern shops attract customers with their unique textured appearance of their store fronts.

The Combination Style

The combination style, an expression of the multiversity of modern design, came about after Post-Modernism. It is not critical of rationalism as Post-Modernism is, and does not worship tradition like Neo-Classicism does. It prefers modern practicality with some elements of tradition. The combination style is a typical 'taking in' style. It may well put a traditional screen behind a modern sofa, decorate the modern-styled doors and windows with classical patterns, or put the European classical glazed lamp on a traditional Chinese tea table. The combination style does not stick to one style, but combine different methods, styles and theories to reach a universal harmony among spaces, colours and materials. Thus, there is no uniformity in its colour design and has generally more contrasts and conflicts.

← Traditional Chinese costumes versus paintings from the Bible and classical furniture versus modern glass tea tables-a paradox or a conflict?

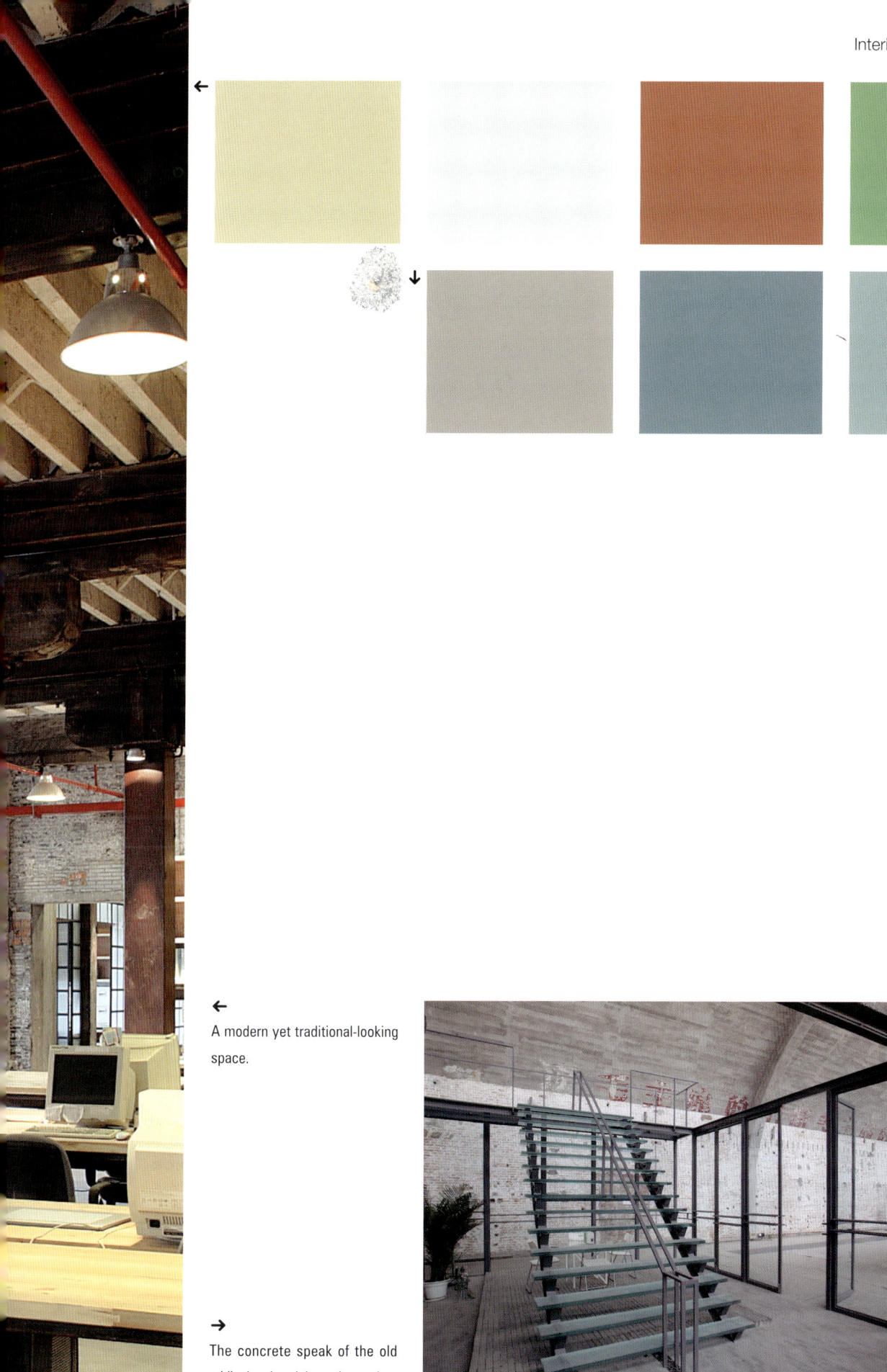

←

A modern yet traditional-looking space.

→

The concrete speak of the old while the glass injects the modern beat of life into the space.

combination of classical chairs,
een trees, modern bricks and
ditional carpets.

First published in 2006 by Page One Publishing Private Limited
2nd edition 2007

Published in 2007 by:
Page One Publishing Private Limited
20 Kaki Bukit View
Kaki Bukit Techpark II
Singapore 415956
Tel: (65) 6742-2088
Fax: (65) 6744-2088
enquiries@pageonegroup.com
www.pageonegroup.com

Distributed by:
Page One Publishing Private Limited
20 Kaki Bukit View
Kaki Bukit Techpark II
Singapore 415956
Tel: (65) 6742-2088
Fax: (65) 6744-2088

Chief Editor: Chen Ci Liang
Cover Design: Benjamin Cheh
English Text: Lynette Wan

ISBN: 978-981-245-344-0

Printed and bound by:
SNP Leefung Printers (Shen Zhen) Co. Ltd.